Thomas Arnold, John Dryden

An Essay of Dramatic Poesy

Thomas Arnold, John Dryden

An Essay of Dramatic Poesy

ISBN/EAN: 9783337337438

Printed in Europe, USA, Canada, Australia, Japan

Cover: Foto ©Thomas Meinert / pixelio.de

More available books at **www.hansebooks.com**

Clarendon Press Series

DRYDEN

AN ESSAY OF DRAMATIC POESY

EDITED WITH NOTES

BY

THOMAS ARNOLD, M.A.

OF UNIV. COLL., OXFORD
FELLOW OF THE ROYAL UNIVERSITY OF IRELAND

SECOND EDITION

Oxford

AT THE CLARENDON PRESS

M DCCC XCVI

Oxford
PRINTED AT THE CLARENDON PRESS
BY HORACE HART, PRINTER TO THE UNIVERSITY

PREFACE.

It is interesting to note that the same cause—the great plague of 1665—which drove Milton from London to the Buckinghamshire village of Chalfont St. Giles, and there gave him leisure to complete the *Paradise Lost*, obliged Dryden also—the theatres being closed—to pass eighteen months in the country,—'probably at Charlton in Wiltshire,' says Malone,—where he turned his leisure to so good an account as, besides writing the 'Annus Mirabilis,' to compose in the following Essay the first piece of good modern English prose on which our literature can pride itself.

Charles II, having been much in Paris during his exile, had been captivated by the French drama, then in the powerful hands of Corneille and Molière. In that drama, when prose was not employed, the use of rhyme was an essential feature.

Dryden and others were not slow to consult the taste prevailing at Court. His first play, *The Wild Gallant*, was in prose; it is coarse and not much enlivened by wit, and it was not well received. In his next efforts Dryden took greater pains. He seems to have convinced himself that the attraction of rhyme was necessary to please the fastidious audiences for which he had to write;

and after *The Rival Ladies*, which is partly in rhyme partly in blank verse,—and *The Indian Queen* (1664), a play entirely rhymed, in which he assisted his brother-in-law Sir Robert Howard,—he brought out, early in 1665, his tragedy of *The Indian Emperor*, which, like *The Indian Queen*, is carefully rhymed throughout. In the enforced leisure which his residence at Charlton during the plague brought him, he thought over the whole subject, and this *Essay of Dramatic Poesy* was the result.

In the course of time Dryden modified more or less the judgment in favour of rhyme which he had given in the *Essay*. In the prologue to the tragedy of *Aurungzebe, or the Great Mogul* (1675), he says that he finds it more difficult to please himself than his audience, and is inclined to damn his own play :—

> Not that it's worse than what before he writ,
> But he has now another taste of wit;
> And, to confess a truth. though out of time,
> Grows weary of his long-loved mistress, Rhyme.

Passion, he proceeds, is too fierce to be bound in fetters; and the sense of Shakspere's unapproachable superiority, —Shakspere, whose masterpieces dispense with rhyme,— inclines him to quit the stage altogether. Nevertheless his original contention,—however under the pressure of dejection, and the sense perhaps of flagging powers, he may afterwards have been willing to abandon it,—cannot be lightly set aside as either weak or unimportant ; a point on which I shall have something to say presently.

Five critical questions are handled in the Essay, viz.—

1. The relative merits of ancient and modern poets.

2. Whether the existing French school of drama is superior or inferior to the English.

3. Whether the Elizabethan dramatists were in all points superior to those of Dryden's own time.

4. Whether plays are more perfect in proportion as they conform to the dramatic rules laid down by the ancients.

5. Whether the substitution of rhyme for blank verse in serious plays is an improvement.

The first point is considered in the remarks of Crites (Sir Robert Howard), with which the discussion opens. In connexion with it the speaker deals with the fourth point, assuming without proof that regard to the unities of Time and Place, inasmuch as it tends to heighten the illusion of reality, must place the authors who pay it above those who neglect it. Eugenius (Lord Buckhurst) answers him, pointing out the narrow range of the Greek drama, and several defects which its greatest admirers cannot deny. Crites makes a brief reply, and then Lisideius (Sir Charles Sedley) plunges into the second question, and ardently maintains that the French theatre, which was formerly inferior to ours, now,—since it had been ennobled by the rise of Corneille and his fellow-workers, —surpasses it and the rest of Europe. This commendation he grounds partly on their exact observance of the dramatic rules, partly on their exclusion of undue complication from their plots and general regard to the ' decorum of the stage,' partly also on the beauty of their rhyme. Neander (Dryden) takes up the defence of the English stage, and tries to show that it is superior to the

French at every point. 'For the verse itself,' he says, 'we have English precedents of older date than any of Corneille's plays.' By 'verse' he means rhyme. He is not rash enough to quote *Gammer Gurton's Needle* and similar plays, with their hobbling twelve-syllable couplets, as 'precedents' earlier than the graceful French Alexandrines, but he urges that Shakspere in his early plays has long rhyming passages, and that Jonson is not without them. At this point Eugenius breaks in with the question, Whether Ben Jonson ought not to rank before all other writers, both French and English. Before undertaking to decide this point, Neander says that he will attempt to estimate the dramatic genius of Shakspere, and of Beaumont and Fletcher. This he does, in an interesting and well-known passage (p. 67). He then examines the genius of Jonson with reference to many special points, and gives an analysis of the plot of his comedy, *Epicene, or the Silent Woman*; but he gives no direct answer to the question put by Eugenius. To the English stage as a whole he will not allow a position of inferiority; for 'our nation can never want in any age such who are able to dispute the empire of wit with any people in the universe.'

Crites now introduces the subject of rhyme, which he maintains to be unsuitable for serious plays. His argument, and Neander's answer, take up the rest of the Essay.

The personages who conduct the discussion are all of a social rank higher than that to which Dryden belonged. Sir Robert Howard, the son of the Earl of Berkshire, assumed the poet's lyre or the critic's stylus with an air of superiority which showed that he thought it a real condescension in himself, a man of fashion, to herd with the poverty-stricken tribe of authors. This tone is very noticeable in the Preface to *The Duke of Lerma*, which Dryden answered in his *Defence of the Essay*. Sir Charles Sedley was a well-known Kentish baronet, and Lord Buckhurst, soon to be the Earl of Dorset, was heir to the illustrious house of Sackville. It is perhaps in contrast to the social distinction of his friends that Dryden modestly calls himself 'Neander,' which may be taken to represent 'novus homo,' a man of the people, desiring to rise above his station.

This question as to the value of rhyme in dramatic poetry is by no means an obsolete or unprofitable inquiry; it still exercises our minds in the nineteenth century; it has received no permanent, no authoritative solution. It is usually assumed that Dryden was altogether wrong in preferring the heroic couplet to blank verse as the metre of serious dramas; and his own subsequent abandonment of rhyme—foreshadowed, as we have seen, in the prologue to *Aurung-zebe*—is regarded as an admission that his argument in favour of it was unsound. And yet much of what he says in defence of rhyme appears to be plain common sense and incontrovertible, and to deserve, whatever his later practice may have been, a careful consideration. After all, if the heroic rhyming plays of Dryden, Lee, and Etherege have found no successors, has not blank verse also notoriously failed, however able the hands which wielded it, to become the vehicle and instrument of an English dramatic school, worthy to be ranked alongside of the great Elizabethans? Since Dryden's, the only supremely excellent plays which English literature has produced are Sheridan's; and these are comedies, and in prose. Coleridge, Young, Addison, Byron, Shelley, Lytton-Bulwer,—all attempted tragedy in blank verse; and none of their tragedies can be said to live. The fact is, that the amazing superiority of Shakspere, lying much more in the matter than in the form of his tragedies, makes us ready to admit at once that blank verse is the proper metre for an English tragedy because he used it. We do not see that the *ensemble* of the facts of the case,—viz. that no Elizabethan blank verse tragedy, *besides* those of Shakspere, can be endured on the stage now, and that those of later dramatists have not been successful,—might lead us to the conclusion that Shakspere triumphed rather *in spite of* blank verse than *because of* it.

Rhyme is merely one of the devices to which the poetic artist has recourse, for the purpose of making his work attractive and successful. Whether we take style, or metre, or quantity, or rhyme, the source of the pleasure seems to be always the same,—it lies in the victory of that which is formed over the formless, of the orderly over the anarchic,—in the substitution of Cosmos for Chaos,—in the felt contrast between the flat and bald converse of common life, and the measured and coloured speech of the orator or poet. Style belongs to prose: metre, quantity, and rhyme to poetry. Metre is the arrangement of the words and syllables of a composition into equal or equivalent lengths, the regular and expected recurrence of which is the source of a peculiar pleasure. Quantity is an improvement which can only have sprung up among those whose ears had long been trained in the strict observance of metre. By Quantity is meant the volume, or time, or weight of a syllable. A 'false quantity' consists in giving to a syllable a sound larger, longer, and heavier,—or on the other hand smaller, shorter, and lighter,—than that which the ear expects. It is obvious that constant study and observation would tend to determine the quantity of all syllables which it was possible to use in poetry; and not their natural quantity only, i. e. the weight which they had when standing alone, but also the quantity given them by their position before other syllables. This work of quantifying—as it may be called—after being carried to great perfection among the Greeks, was by them imparted to the Romans. Then it was that, 'horridus ille Defluxit numerus Saturnius,' the rough stumbling measure of Naevius and earlier poets went into disuse, and metre perfected by quantity, in the various moulds,—hexameter, elegiac, alcaic, &c.,—which Greek invention had created, took its place.

Crites rightly extols the metre and quantity of the ancients; his mistake is in inferring, because the ancients did not use rhyme, that therefore it should be eschewed by the moderns. Neander, or Dryden, states correctly enough that when Roman society was broken up, and the Latin tongue, upon the invasions of the Barbarians, had become corrupted into several vernacular dialects, whence gradually emerged the new languages of southern Europe, the niceties of quantity were obscured or forgotten, and some new attraction was felt to be necessary by the poetic artist in order to supply its place.   This attraction was found in rhyme.

Attraction may however be studied too exclusively; there may be too much ornament as well as too little. Poetry, by presenting ideas in a beautiful dress, aims at making them loved.   But the ideas themselves are the main consideration, and if the dress is too much obtruded,—if it attract attention for its own sake and not for the sake of what it clothes, a fault is committed, and a failure incurred.   As Aristotle considered (*Poet.* IV) that the elaborate Greek metres were unsuited for tragedy, and that the iambic trimeter, as 'nearer to common discourse,' was its proper instrument, so it is quite possible that in modern dramatic verse rhyme may fix the attention too much upon the *manner* of saying a thing, when the thing itself ought to concentrate upon it the thoughts and feelings of the spectators.   But this extreme, owing to the difficulty and toil which finding rhymes imposes on the author, is less often met than its opposite.   For one rhyming play which errs by excess of ornament, there are ten plays in blank verse which err by being flat and dull.   Shakspere in his best plays observes the true mean, making his blank verse so rhythmic and beautiful that the hearer requires no other ornament; while by rejecting rhyme he avoids the danger of weakening that interest which should be excited by the plot and the characters.   When such blank verse as the following can be had, no one will ever ask for rhyme :—

> Forbear to sleep the night, and fast the day,
> Compare dead happiness with living woe ;
> Think that thy babes were fairer than they were,
> And him that slew them fouler than he is ;
> Bettering thy loss makes the bad causer worse;
> Revolving this will teach thee how to curse.

But when long passages are given us such as—

> There is no vice so simple but assumes
> Some mark of virtue on his outward parts:
> How many cowards, whose hearts are all as false
> As stairs of sand, wear yet upon their chins
> The beards of Hercules and frowning Mars,
> Who, inward search'd, have livers white as milk ;
> And these assume but valour's excrement
> To render them redoubted, &c., &c.—

then, since the thoughts are neither supremely interesting in themselves, nor presented with supreme force or skill, the hearer is apt to grow weary, and to ask from the form of the verse that entertainment which he does not derive from the substance. In other words, he would, consciously or not, be glad of rhyme if he could get it.

There seems good reason to think that the French masterpieces of the seventeenth century would not, if they were not rhymed, hold their ground on the modern stage. With us, Shakspere's amazing genius enables us, even without the aid of rhyme, still to enjoy his plays ; but this is true of no other dramatist of that age [1]. In his work on the Elizabethan dramatists, Charles Lamb produced passages from some of the best plays of all the

[1] Massinger's *New Way to pay Old Debts* is perhaps the only exception to the statement in the text.

principal authors; but it must be owned that they make no great impression. For this there are indeed other causes;—the wit is not such as amuses at the present day; the passion is rather Italian or Spanish than English;—but it is also true that the story is seldom sufficiently interesting, or the thoughts sufficiently striking, to enchain our attention for their own sakes, apart from the pleasure given by rhyme. On the other hand, in reading such a collection as Mr. Palgrave's *Golden Treasury*, all of us are conscious of the continued presence of pleasurable feeling. What reason can be found for this difference of impression, except that rhyme,—and often exquisitely managed rhyme,—is present throughout Mr. Palgrave's collection, and absent throughout Lamb's collection? If the English serious drama, expressed in blank verse, had continued to make progress from the beginning of the seventeenth century, and were in a flourishing condition at the present time, Dryden's plea for rhyme, since it might seem to have been disproved by the event, might well be rejected. But the English serious drama[1] at this moment is in such a low condition as to be almost non-existent. It seems therefore to be a question open to argument whether, in spite of the success,—due to exceptional power,—of *Hamlet* or *King Lear*, Dryden was not right in holding that the average dramatist could not safely dispense, if he wished permanently to please English audiences, with the music and the charm of rhyme.

[1] Of course I am not speaking of chamber pieces, but of plays intended for the stage.

The *Defence of the Essay of Dramatic Poesy* appeared later in the same year, 1668. After the publication of the Essay, Sir Robert Howard printed his tragedy of *The Duke of Lerma*, in the preface to which (printed by Malone in his collected edition of Dryden's prose works) he attacked with blundering vehemence the poet's argument on behalf of rhyme. Dryden seems to have been much nettled, and in this sharp and masterly reply he exposes the blunders, and makes short work of the arguments, of his brother-in-law. This *Defence* was prefixed to the second edition, just at that time called for, of *The Indian Emperor*. But Dryden must have been unwilling for many reasons to let this passage of arms ripen into a formal quarrel. From later editions of *The Indian Emperor* he suppressed the preface, and forbore ever to publish it in a separate form. It was not again printed till after his death.

Three editions of the *Essay of Dramatic Poesy* were published in the author's lifetime; see page 8. Since 1700 it has been three times reprinted; first by Robert Urie in his *Select Essays on the Belles Lettres*, Glasgow, 1750; secondly, by Malone in his edition of Dryden's prose works (1800); and lastly, by Sir Walter Scott in his general edition of all Dryden's works, published in 1808 [1].

[1] And now in course of republication under the superintendence of Mr. Saintsbury.

EPISTLE DEDICATORY

TO THE ESSAY OF

DRAMATIC POESY[1].

——•+——

TO THE RIGHT HONOURABLE

CHARLES, LORD BUCKHURST[2].

MY LORD,

As I was lately reviewing my loose papers,
amongst the rest I found this Essay, the writing of
which, in this rude and indigested manner wherein
your lordship now sees it, served as an amusement 5
to me in the country, when the violence of the last
plague[3] had driven me from the town. Seeing then
our theatres shut up, I was engaged in these kind
of thoughts with the same delight with which men
think upon their absent mistresses. I confess I find 10
many things in this Discourse which I do not now
approve; my judgment being not a little altered[4]

---

[1] A = edition of 1668. B = edition of 1684 (here, in the main,
reprinted). C = edition of 1693.

[2] C has, 'Charles Earl of Dorset and Middlesex, Lord Chamberlain
of their Majesties Houshold, Knight of the Most Noble Order of
the Garter, &c.' Lord Buckhurst had become Earl of Dorset in 1677.
It is hard to say why Dryden did not give him his proper title in the
edition of 1684.

[3] The great plague of 1665 (Malone).   [4] a little altered, A.

B

since the writing of it; but whether[1] for the better or the worse, I know not: neither indeed is it much material, in an essay, where all I have said is problematical. For the way of writing plays in verse,
5 which I have seemed to favour, I have, since that time, laid the practice of it aside, till I have more leisure, because I find it troublesome and slow. But I am no way altered from my opinion of it, at least with any reasons which have opposed it. For your lord-
10 ship may easily observe, that none are very violent against it, but those who either have not attempted it, or who have succeeded ill in their attempt. It is enough for me to have your lordship's example for my excuse in that little which I have done in it;
15 and I am sure my adversaries can bring no such arguments against verse, as those with which the fourth act of *Pompey* will furnish me[2] in its defence. Yet, my lord, you must suffer me a little to complain of you, that you too soon withdraw from us a con-
20 tentment, of which we expected the continuance, because you gave it us so early. It is a revolt, without occasion, from your party, where your merits had already raised you to the highest commands, and where you have not the excuse of other men, that
25 you have been ill used, and therefore laid down arms[3]. I know no other quarrel you can have to verse, than that[4] which Spurina[n] had to his beauty, when he tore and mangled the features of his face, only[5] because they pleased too well the sight[6]. It

---

[1] whither, A.
[2] as the fourth Act of *Pompey* will furnish me with, A.
[3] Armes, A.   [4] then that, A.   [5] onely, A.   [6] the lookers on, A.

was an honour which seemed to wait for you, to lead
out a new colony of writers from the mother nation :
and upon the first spreading of your ensigns, there
had been many in a readiness to have followed so
fortunate a leader ; if not all, yet the better part of [5]
poets [1] :

> —— *pars, indocili melior grege; mollis et cxspes* [2]
> *Inominata perprimat cubilia.* [n]

I am almost of opinion, that we should force you to
accept of the command, as sometimes the Praetorian [10]
bands have compelled their captains to receive the
empire. The court, which is the best and surest
judge of writing, has generally allowed [n] of verse ;
and in the town it has found favourers of wit and
quality. As for your own particular, my lord, you [15]
have yet youth and time enough to give part of
them [3] to the divertisement of the public, before you
enter into the serious and more unpleasant business
of the world. That which the French poet said of
the temple of Love, may be as well applied to the [20]
temple of the Muses. The words, as near as I can
remember them, were these :

> *Le jeune homme à mauvaise grace,*
> *N'ayant pas adoré dans le Temple d'Amour;*
> *Il faut qu'il entre ; et pour le sage,*   [25]
> *Si ce n'est pas son vrai* [4] *sejour,*
> *C'est un gîte* [5] *sur son passage.* [n]

I leave the words to work their effect upon your
lordship in their own language, because no other can
so well express the nobleness of the thought ; and [30]
wish you may be soon called to bear a part in the

---

[1] Writers, A.   [2] *expes*, A.   [3] of it, A.
[4] Si ce nest son vray, A.   [5] Ce'st un giste, A.

affairs of the nation, where I know the world expects you, and wonders why you have been so long forgotten; there being no person amongst our young nobility, on whom the eyes of all men are so much 5 bent. But in the mean time, your lordship may imitate the course of Nature, who gives us the flower before the fruit : that I may speak to you in the language of the muses, which I have taken from an excellent poem to the king :

10
> As Nature, when she fruit designs[1], thinks fit
> By beauteous blossoms to proceed to it ;
> And while she does accomplish all the spring,
> Birds to her secret operations sing.[n]

I confess I have no greater reason, in addressing 15 this Essay to your lordship, than that it might awaken in you the desire of writing something, in whatever kind it be, which might be an honour to our age and country. And methinks it might have the same effect on you, which Homer tells us the 20 fight of the Greeks and Trojans before the fleet, had on the spirit of Achilles; who, though he had resolved not to engage[2], yet found a martial warmth to steal upon him at the sight of blows, the sound of trumpets, and the cries of fighting men.

25 For my own part, if, in treating of this subject, I sometimes dissent from the opinion of better wits, I declare it is not so much to combat their opinions, as to defend my own, which were first made publick.[n] Sometimes, like a scholar in a fencing-school, I put 30 forth myself, and shew my own ill play, on purpose to be better taught. Sometimes I stand desperately to

---

[1] designes, A.   [2] ingage, A.

my arms, like the foot when deserted by their horse ;
not in hope to overcome, but only to yield on more
honourable terms. And yet, my lord, this war of
opinions, you well know, has fallen out among the
writers of all ages, and sometimes betwixt friends. 5
Only it has been prosecuted by some, like pedants,
with violence of words, and managed by others like
gentlemen, with candour and civility. Even Tully
had a controversy with his dear Atticus ; and in one
of his Dialogues, makes him sustain the part of an 10
enemy in philosophy, who, in his letters, is his confident of state, and made privy to the most weighty
affairs of the Roman senate. And the same respect
which was paid by Tully to Atticus, we find returned
to him afterwards by Caesar on a like occasion, who 15
answering his book in praise of Cato, made it not so
much his business to condemn Cato, as to praise
Cicero. [n]

But that I may decline some part of the encounter
with my adversaries, whom I am neither willing to 20
combat, nor well able to resist; I will give your
lordship the relation of a dispute betwixt some of our
wits on the same subject [1], in which they did not only
speak of plays in verse, but mingled, in the freedom
of discourse, some things of the ancient, many of the 25
modern, ways of writing ; comparing those with these,
and the wits of our nation with those of others : it is
true [2], they differed in their opinions, as it is probable [3]
they would : neither do I take upon me to reconcile,
but to relate them ; and that as Tacitus professes of 30

---

[1] upon this subject, A.   [2] 'tis true, A.

[3] 'tis probable, A.

himself, *sine studio partium, aut irâ*[1], without passion
or interest ; leaving your lordship to decide it in
favour of which part you shall judge most reasonable,
and withal, to pardon the many errors of

5   Your Lordship's

            Most obedient humble servant,

                    JOHN DRYDEN.

[1] Tac. Ann. I. 1 ; sine ira aut studio, quorum causas procul habeo

TO THE READER.

THE drift of the ensuing discourse was chiefly to vindicate the honour of our English writers, from the censure of those who unjustly prefer the French before them. This I intimate, lest any should think me so exceeding vain, [n] as to teach others an art which they understand much better than myself. But if this incorrect Essay, written in the country without the help of books or advice of friends, shall find any acceptance in the world, I promise to myself a better success of the Second Part, wherein I shall more fully treat of[1] the virtues and faults of the English poets, who have written either in this, the epick[2], or the lyrick[3] way[4].

---

[1] A *om.* I shall more fully treat of.   [2] Epique, A.

[3] Lyrique, A.

[4] A has, 'will be more fully treated of, and their several styles impartially imitated.'

AN ESSAY

OF

DRAMATIC POESY[1].

———••———

It was that memorable day[2], in the first summer of
5 the late war, when our navy engaged[3] the Dutch; a
day wherein the two most mighty and best appointed
fleets which any age had ever seen, disputed the command of the greater half of the globe, the commerce
of nations, and the riches of the universe: while[4]
10 these vast floating bodies, on either side, moved
against each other in parallel lines, and our countrymen, under the happy conduct of his royal high-
ness[5], went breaking, by little and little, into the
line of the enemies; the noise of the cannon
15 from both navies reached our ears about the city, [n]
so that all men being alarmed with it, and in a dread-
ful suspense of the event, which they knew[6] was then
deciding, every one went following the sound as his
fancy led him; and leaving the town almost empty,

---

[1] Dramatick Poesie, A.   [2] June 3, 1665 (Malone).
[3] ingag'd, A.   [4] Universe. While, A.
[5] James, duke of York, afterwards James II (Malone).
[6] we knew, A.

some took towards the park, some cross the river,
others down it; all seeking the noise in the depth of
silence.

Among the rest, it was the fortune of Eugenius,
Crites, Lisideius, and Neander, to be in company 5
together; three of them persons whom their wit and
quality have made known to all the town; and whom
I have chose to hide under these borrowed names,
that they may not suffer by so ill a relation as I am
going to make of their discourse.   10

2. Taking then a barge, which a servant of Lisideius
had provided for them, they made haste to shoot the
bridge, and left behind them that great fall of waters
which hindered them from hearing what they desired:
after which, having disengaged[1] themselves from many 15
vessels which rode at anchor in the Thames, and almost blocked[2] up the passage towards Greenwich, they
ordered the watermen to let fall their oars more gently;
and then, every one favouring his own curiosity with a
strict silence, it was not long ere they perceived the air 20
to break[3] about them like the noise of distant thunder,
or of swallows in a chimney: those little undulations
of sound, though almost vanishing before they reached
them, yet still seeming to retain somewhat of their
first horrour, which they had betwixt the fleets. 25
After[4] they had attentively listened till such time as
the sound by little and little went from them, Eugenius,
lifting up his head, and taking notice of it, was the
first who congratulated to the rest that happy omen
of our nation's victory: adding, that[5] we had but 30

---

[1] disingag'd, A.   [2] blockt, A.   [3] The Air to break, A.
[4] Fleets: after.   [5] A om.

this to desire in confirmation of it, that we might hear no more of that noise, which was now leaving the English coast. When the rest had concurred in the same opinion, Crites, a person of a sharp judg-
5 ment, and somewhat too delicate a taste in wit, which the world have mistaken in him for ill-nature, said, smiling to us, that if the concernment of this battle[1] had not been so exceeding great, he could scarce have wished the victory at the price he knew he
10 must pay for it, in being subject to the reading and hearing of so many ill verses as he was sure would be made on that subject. Adding[2], that no argument could scape some of those eternal rhymers, who watch a battle with more diligence than the ravens
15 and birds of prey; and the worst of them surest to be first in upon the quarry: while the better able, either out of modesty writ not at all, or set that due value upon their poems, as to let them be often desired[3] and long expected. 'There[4] are some of
20 those impertinent people of whom you speak[5],' answered Lisideius, 'who to my knowledge are already so provided, either way, that they can produce not only a panegyrick upon the victory, but, if need be, a funeral elegy on the duke; wherein, after[6] they have
25 crowned his valour with many laurels, they will[7] at last deplore the odds under which he fell, concluding that his courage deserved a better destiny.' All the company smiled at the conceipt of Lisideius; but Crites, more eager than before, began to make par-

---

[1] battel, A.   [2] upon it; adding, A.   [3] call'd for.
[4] expected! there, A.   [5] people you speak of, A.
[6] and after, A.   [7] A *om.* they will.

ticular exceptions against some writers, and said, the publick magistrate ought to send betimes to forbid them; and that it concerned the peace and quiet of all honest people, that ill poets should be as well silenced as seditious preachers.ⁿ 'In my opinion,' 5 replied Eugenius, 'you pursue your point too far; for as to my own particular, I am so great a lover of poesy, that I could wish them all rewarded, who attempt but to do well; at least, I would not have them worse used than one of their brethren 10 was by Sylla the Dictator[1]:—*Quem in concione vidimus* (says Tully,) *cum ei libellum malus poeta de populo subjecisset, quod epigramma in eum fecisset tantummodo alternis versibus longiusculis, statim ex iis rebus quas tunc[2] vendebat jubere ei praemium tribui, sub* 15 *ea conditione ne quid postea scriberet.'* ⁿ 'I could wish with all my heart,' replied Crites, 'that many whom we know were as bountifully thanked upon the same condition,—that they would never trouble us again. For amongst others, I have a mortal apprehension 20 of two poetsⁿ, whom this victory, with the help of both her wings, will never be able to escape.' ''Tis easy[3] to guess whom you intend,' said Lisideius; 'and without naming them, I ask you, if one of them does not perpetually pay us with 25 clenches upon words, and a certain clownish kind of raillery? if now and then he does not offer at a catachresis[4] or Clevelandism[5], wresting and tor-

---

[1] then [than] Sylla the Dictator did one of their brethren heretofore, A.

[2] quae tunc, A.   [3] escape; 'tis easie, A.

[4] Catecresis, A.   [5] so A; Cleivelandism B, and edd.

turing a word into another meaning: in fine, if he be not one of those whom the French would call *un mauvais buffon*; one who is so much a well-willer to the satire, that he intends at least to spare[1] no
5 man; and though he cannot strike a blow to hurt any, yet he ought[2] to be punished for the malice of the action, as our witches are justly hanged, because they think themselves to be such[3]; and suffer deservedly for believing they did mischief,
10 because they meant it.' 'You have described him,' said Crites, 'so exactly, that I am afraid to come after you with my other extremity of poetry. He is one of those who, having had some advantage of education and converse, knows better than the other
15 what a poet should be, but puts it into practice more unluckily than any man; his style and matter are every where alike: he is the most calm, peaceable writer you ever read: he never disquiets your passions with the least concernment, but still leaves you
20 in as even a temper as he found you; he is a very leveller in poetry: he creeps along with ten little words in every line[4], and helps out his numbers with *For to*, and *Unto*, and all the pretty expletives he can find, till he drags them to the end of another line;
25 while the sense is left tired half way behind it: he doubly starves all his verses, first for want of thought,

---

[1] he spares, A.   [2] yet ought, A.

[3] think themselves so, A.

[4] This passage evidently furnished Pope with his well-known couplet in the ESSAY ON CRITICISM;

 'While *expletives* their feeble aid do join,
 And *ten low words* oft *creep* in one dull line.'

(Malone.)

and then of expression; his poetry neither has wit in it, nor seems to have it; like him in Martial:[n]

Pauper videri Cinna *vult, et est pauper.*

'He affects plainness, to cover his want of imagination: when he writes the serious way, the highest 5 flight of his fancy is some miserable antithesis, or seeming contradiction; and in the comic he is still reaching at some thin conceit, the ghost of a jest, and that too flies before him, never to be caught; these swallows which we see before us on the Thames are 10 the just resemblance of his wit: you may observe how near the water they stoop, how many proffers they make to dip, and yet how seldom they touch it; and when they do, it is but the surface: they skim over it but to catch a gnat, and then mount into the 15 air and leave it.'

3. 'Well, gentlemen,' said Eugenius, 'you may speak your pleasure of these authors; but though I and some few more about the town may give you a peaceable hearing, yet assure yourselves, there are 20 multitudes who would think you malicious and them injured: especially him whom you first described; he is the very Withers[n] of the city: they have bought more editions of his works than would serve to lay under all their pies at the lord mayor's 25 Christmas. When his famous poem first came out in the year 1660, I have seen them reading it in the midst of 'Change time; nay so vehement they were at it, that they lost their bargain by the candles' ends[n]; but what will you say, if he has been re- 30 ceived amongst great persons[1]? I can assure you

[1] the great Ones, A.

he is, this day, the envy of one[1] who is lord in the
art of quibbling; and who does not take it well, that
any man should intrude so far into his province.'
'All I would wish,' replied Crites, 'is, that they who
5 love his writings, may still admire him, and his
fellow poet: *Qui Bavium non odit, &c.,* is curse sufficient.' 'And farther,' added Lisideius, 'I believe
there is no man who writes well, but would think he
had hard measure[2], if their admirers should praise
10 anything of his: *Nam quos contemnimus, eorum quoque laudes contemnimus.'* 'There are so few who
write well in this age,' says Crites, 'that methinks any
praises should be welcome; they neither rise to the
dignity of the last age, nor to any of the ancients:
15 and we may cry out of the writers of this time, with
more reason than Petronius of his, *Pace vestrâ liceat
dixisse, primi omnium eloquentiam perdidistis:*[n] you
have debauched the true old poetry so far, that
Nature, which is the soul of it, is not in any of your
20 writings.'

  4. 'If your quarrel,' said Eugenius, 'to those who
now write, be grounded only on your reverence to
antiquity, there is no man more ready to adore those
great Greeks and Romans than I am: but on the
25 other side, I cannot think so contemptibly of the age
in which I live[3], or so dishonourably of my own
country, as not to judge we equal the ancients in
most kinds of poesy, and in some surpass them;
neither know I any reason why I may not be as

---

[1] of a great person, A.
[2] think himself very hardly dealt with, A.
[3] the Age I live in, A.

zealous for the reputation of our age, as we find the ancients themselves were in reference to those who lived before them. For you hear your Horace saying,

> *Indignor quidquam reprehendi, non quia crassé*   5
> *Compositum, illepidève putetur, sed quia nuper.* [a]

And after:

> *Si meliora dies, ut vina, potmata reddit,*
> *Scire velim, pretium chartis quotus arroget annus?* [a]

'But I see I am engaging in a wide dispute, where 10 the arguments are not like to reach close on either side; for poesy is of so large an extent, and so many both of the ancients and moderns have done well in all kinds of it, that in citing one against the other, we shall take up more time this evening than each 15 man's occasions [1] will allow him: therefore I would ask Crites to what part of poesy he would confine his arguments, and whether he would defend the general cause of the ancients against the moderns, or oppose any age of the moderns against this of 20 ours?'

5. Crites, a little while considering upon this de-mand, told Eugenius, that if [2] he pleased, he would limit their dispute to Dramatique Poesie [3]; in which he thought it not difficult to prove, either that the 25 ancients were superior to the moderns, or the last age to this of ours.

Eugenius was somewhat surprised, when he heard Crites make choice of that subject. 'For ought I

---

[1] so C; mans occasions, A, B.
[2] that he approv'd his Proposals, and if, **A.**
[3] so A and B; Dramatick Poesie, C.

see,' said he, 'I have undertaken a harder province
than I imagined; for though I never judged the
plays of the Greek or Roman poets comparable to
ours, yet, on the other side, those we now see acted
5 come short of many which were written in the last
age: but my comfort is, if we are overcome, it will
be only by our own countrymen: and if we yield to
them in this one part of poesy, we more surpass
them in all the other: for in the epic or lyric way, it
10 will be hard for them to shew us one such amongst
them, as we have many now living, or who lately
were[1]: they can produce nothing so courtly writ, or
which expresses so much the conversation of a
gentleman, as Sir John Suckling; nothing so even,
15 sweet, and flowing, as Mr. Waller; nothing so majestic,
so correct, as Sir John Denham; nothing so elevated,
so copious, and full of spirit, as Mr. Cowley; as
for the Italian, French, and Spanish plays, I can
make it evident, that those who now write surpass
20 them; and that the drama is wholly ours.'

All of them were thus far of Eugenius his[n] opinion,
that the sweetness of English verse was never understood or practised by our fathers; even Crites himself did not much oppose it: and every one was
25 willing to acknowledge how much our poesy is im-
proved by the happiness of some writers yet living;
who first taught us to mould our thoughts into easy
and significant words,—to retrench the superfluities
of expression,—and to make our rime[2] so properly a
30 part of the verse, that it should never mislead the
sense, but itself be led and governed by it.

---

[1] were so, A.   [2] so A and B; rhyme, C.

6. Eugenius was going to continue this discourse, when Lisideius told him that[1] it was necessary, before they proceeded further, to take a standing measure of their controversy; for how was it possible to be decided who writ the best plays, before we know 5 what a play should be? But, this once agreed on by both parties, each might have recourse to it, either to prove his own advantages, or to discover the failings of his adversary.

He had no sooner said this, but all desired the 10 favour of him to give the definition of a play; and they were the more importunate, because neither Aristotle, nor Horace, nor any other, who had writ[2] of that subject, had ever done it.

Lisideius, after some modest denials, at last con- 15 fessed he had a rude notion of it; indeed, rather a description than a definition; but which served to guide him in his private thoughts, when he was to make a judgment of what others writ: that he conceived a play ought to be, *A just and lively image of* 20 *human nature, representing its passions and humours, and the changes of fortune to which it is subject, for the delight and instruction of mankind.*

This definition, though Crites raised a logical objection against it—that it was only *a genere et fine*, 25 and so not altogether perfect [n], was yet well received by the rest: and after they had given order to the watermen to turn their barge, and row softly, that they might take the cool of the evening in their return, Crites, being desired by the company to begin, 30 spoke on behalf of the ancients, in this manner:—

---

[1] A *om.*   [2] who writ, A.

C

'If confidence presage a victory, Eugenius, in his own opinion, has already triumphed over the ancients: nothing seems more easy to him, than to overcome those whom it is our greatest praise to 5 have imitated well; for we do not only build upon their foundations[1], but by their models. Dramatic Poesy had time enough, reckoning from Thespis (who first invented it) to Aristophanes, to be born, to grow up, and to flourish in maturity. It has been 10 observed of arts and sciences, that in one and the same century they have arrived to great[2] perfection;[n] and no wonder, since every age has a kind of universal genius, which inclines those that live in it to some particular studies: the work then, being 15 pushed on by many hands, must of necessity go forward.

'Is it not evident, in these last hundred years, when the study of philosophy has been the business of all the Virtuosi in Christendom, that almost a 20 new nature has been revealed to us? That more errors of the school have been detected, more useful experiments in philosophy have been made, more noble secrets in optics, medicine, anatomy, astronomy, discovered, than in all those credulous and 25 doting ages from Aristotle to us?—so true it is, that nothing spreads more fast than science, when rightly and generally cultivated.

'Add to this, the more than common emulation that was in those times of writing well; which 30 though it be found in all ages and all persons that pretend to the same reputation, yet poesy, being

[1] foundation, A.   [2] a great, A.

then in more esteem than now it is, had greater
honours decreed to the professors of it, and consequently the rivalship was more high between them ;
they had judges ordained to decide their merit, and
prizes to reward it ; and historians have been dili- 5
gent to record of Eschylus, Euripides, Sophocles,
Lycophron, and the rest of them, both who they
were that vanquished in these wars of the theatre,
and how often they were crowned : while the Asian
kings and Grecian commonwealths scarce afforded 10
them a nobler subject than the unmanly luxuries of
a debauched court, or giddy intrigues of a factious
city :—*Alit æmulatio ingenia,* (says Paterculus,) *et
nunc invidia, nunc admiratio incitationem accendit :* n
Emulation is the spur of wit ; and sometimes envy, 15
sometimes admiration, quickens our endeavours.

'But now, since the rewards of honour are taken
away, that virtuous emulation is turned into direct
malice ; yet so slothful, that it contents itself to condemn and cry down others, without attempting to do 20
better : it is[1] a reputation too unprofitable, to take
the necessary pains for it ; yet, wishing they had it,
that desire[2] is incitement enough to hinder others
from it. And this, in short, Eugenius, is the reason
why you have now so few good poets, and so many 25
severe judges. Certainly, to imitate the ancients
well, much labour and long study is required ; which
pains, I have already shewn, our poets would want
encouragement to take, if yet they had ability to go
through the work[3]. Those ancients have been faithful 30
imitators and wise observers of that nature which is

---

[1] 'tis, A.   [2] A *om.* that desire.   [3] through with it, A.

so torn and ill represented in our plays; they have
handed down to us a perfect resemblance of her;
which we, like ill copiers, neglecting to look on, have
rendered monstrous, and disfigured. But, that you
5 may know how much you are indebted to those your
masters, and be ashamed to have so ill requited
them, I must remember you, that all the rules by
which we practise the drama at this day, (either such
as relate to the justness and symmetry of the plot, or
10 the episodical ornaments, such as descriptions, narrations, and other beauties, which are not essential
to the play[1],) were delivered to us from the observations which Aristotle made, of those poets, who
either lived before him, or were his contemporaries :
15 we have added nothing of our own, except we have
the confidence to say our wit is better; of which,
none boast in this our age, but such as understand
not theirs. Of that book which Aristotle has left us,
περὶ τῆς Ποιητικῆς, Horace his Art of Poetry is an ex-
20 cellent comment, and, I believe, restores to us that
Second Book of his concerning Comedy, which is
wanting in him.[n]

'Out of these two have[2] been extracted the famous
Rules, which the French call *Des Trois Unites*, or,
25 The Three Unities, which ought to be observed in
every regular play; namely, of Time, Place, and
Action.

'The unity of time they comprehend in twenty-four
hours, the compass of a natural day, or as near as it
30 can be contrived; and the reason of it is obvious to
every one,—that the time of the feigned action, or

_____

[1] no brackets in A.   [2] has, A.

fable of the play, should be proportioned as near as can be to the duration of that time in which it is represented: since therefore, all plays are acted on the theatre in the space of time much within the compass of twenty-four hours, that play is to be thought the 5 nearest imitation of nature, whose plot or action is confined within that time; and, by the same rule which concludes this general proportion of time, it follows, that all the parts of it are (as near as may be[1]) to be equally subdivided; namely[2], that one act 10 take not up the supposed time of half a day, which is out of proportion to the rest; since the other four are then to be straitened within the compass of the remaining half: for it is unnatural that one act, which being spoke or written is not longer than the rest, 15 should be supposed longer by the audience; it is therefore the poet's duty, to take care that no act should be imagined to exceed the time in which it is represented on the stage; and that the intervals and inequalities of time be supposed to fall out between 20 the acts.

'This rule of time, how well it has been observed by the ancients, most of their plays will witness; you see them in their tragedies, (wherein to follow this rule, is certainly most difficult,) from the very be- 25 ginning of their plays, falling close into that part of the story which they intend for the action or principal object of it, leaving the former part to be delivered by narration: so that they set the audience, as it were, at the post where the race is to be concluded; and, saving 30 them the tedious expectation of seeing the poet set out

[1] A *om.* as near as may be.   [2] as namely, A.

and ride the beginning of the course, they suffer you
not to behold him[1], till he is in sight of the goal, and
just upon you.

'For the second unity, which is that of Place, the
5 ancients meant by it, that the scene ought to be continued through the play, in the same place where it
was laid in the beginning: for, the stage on which it
is represented being but one and the same place, it is
unnatural to conceive it many,—and those far distant
10 from one another. I will not deny but, by the vari-
ation of painted scenes, the fancy, which in these
cases will contribute to its own deceit, may sometimes
imagine it several places, with some appearance of
probability; yet it still carries the greater likelihood
15 of truth, if those places be supposed so near each
other, as in the same town or city; which may all be
comprehended under the larger denomination of one
place; for a greater distance will bear no proportion
to the shortness of time which is allotted, in the
20 acting, to pass from one of them to another; for the
observation of this, next to the ancients, the French
are to be most commended. They tie themselves so
strictly to the unity of place, that you never see in
any of their plays, a scene changed in the middle of
25 an act: if the act begins in a garden, a street, or
chamber, 'tis ended in the same place; and that you
may know it to be the same, the stage is so supplied
with persons, that it is never empty all the time: he
who enters second[2], has business with him who was
30 on before; and before the second quits the stage,
a third appears who has business with him. This

[1] you behold him not, A.   [2] that enters the second, A.

Corneille[1] calls *la liaison des scenes*, the continuity or
joining of the scenes ; and 'tis a good mark of a well-
contrived play, when all the persons are known to
each other, and every one of them has some affairs
with all the rest.   5

'As for the third unity, which is that of Action, the
ancients meant no other by it than what the logicians
do by their *finis*, the end or scope of any action ; that
which is the first in intention, and last in execution :
now the poet is to aim at one great and complete 10
action, to the carrying on of which all things in his
play, even the very obstacles, are to be subservient ;
and the reason of this is as evident as any of the
former.   For two actions, equally laboured and driven
on by the writer, would destroy the unity of the poem ; 15
it would be no longer one play, but two : not but that
there may be many actions in a play, as Ben Johnson
has observed in his *Discoveries*[11] ; but they must be
all subservient to the great one, which our language
happily expresses in the name of *under-plots* : such as 20
in Terence's *Eunuch* is the difference and reconcile-
ment of Thais and Phædria, which is not the chief
business of the play, but promotes the marriage of
Chærea and Chremes's sister, principally intended
by the poet.   There ought to be but one action, says 25
Corneille, that is, one complete action, which leaves
the mind of the audience in a full repose ; but this
cannot be brought to pass but by many other imperfect actions, which conduce to it, and hold the
audience in a delightful suspence of what will be.   30

'If by these rules (to omit many other drawn from

[1] Corneil, A.

the precepts and practice of the ancients) we should judge our modern plays, 'tis probable that few of them would endure the trial: that which should be the business of a day, takes up in some of them an age;
5 instead of one action, they are the epitomes of a man's life; and for one spot of ground, which the stage should represent, we are sometimes in more countries than the map can shew us.

'But if we allow the Ancients to have contrived
10 well, we must acknowledge them to have written[1] better. Questionless we are deprived of a great stock of wit in the loss of Menander among the Greek poets, and of Cæcilius, Afranius, and Varius, among the Romans; we may guess at Menander's excellency
15 by the plays of Terence, who translated some of his[2]; and yet wanted so much of him, that he was called by C. Cæsar the half-Menander; and may judge[3] of Varius, by the testimonies of Horace, Martial, and Velleius Paterculus. 'Tis probable that these, could
20 they be recovered, would decide the controversy; but so long as Aristophanes and Plautus[4] are extant, while the tragedies of Euripides, Sophocles, and Seneca, are in our hands[5], I can never see one of those plays which are now written, but it increases
25 my admiration of the ancients. And yet I must acknowledge further, that to admire them as we ought, we should understand them better than we do. Doubtless many things appear flat to us, the wit of which[6] depended on some custom or story, which never came

---

[1] writ, A.   [2] so A : B has 'them.'   [3] A *om.* may judge.
[4] Aristophanes in the old Comedy and Plautus in the new, A.
[5] are to be had, A.   [6] whose wit, A.

to our knowledge; or perhaps on some criticism in
their language, which being so long dead, and only
remaining in their books, 'tis not possible they should
make us understand[1] perfectly. To read Macrobius,
explaining the propriety and elegancy of many words 5
in Virgil, which I had before passed over without
consideration as common things, is enough to assure
me that I ought to think the same of Terence; and
that in the purity of his style (which Tully so much
valued that he ever carried his works about him) there 10
is yet left in him great room for admiration, if I knew
but where to place it.   In the mean time I must desire
you to take notice, that the greatest man of the last
age, Ben Johnson, was willing to give place to them in
all things: he was not only a professed imitator of 15
Horace, but a learned plagiary of all the others; you
track him every where in their snow: if Horace, Lucan,
Petronius Arbiter, Seneca, and Juvenal, had their
own from him, there are few serious thoughts which
are new in him: you will pardon me, therefore, if I 20
presume he loved their fashion, when he wore their
cloaths. But since I have otherwise a great veneration for him, and you, Eugenius, prefer him above all
other poets,* I will use no farther argument to you
than his example: I will produce before you Father 25
Ben[2], dressed in all the ornaments and colours of the
ancients; you will need no other guide to our party,
if you follow him; and whether you consider the bad

---

[1] know it, A.   [2] Father Ben to you, A.

* See a high eulogy on Ben Jonson, by Lord Buckhurst (the
Eugenius of this piece), written about the year 1668. Dryden's
MISCEL. v. 123, edit. 1716 (Malone).

plays of our age, or regard the good plays[1] of the
last, both the best and worst of the modern poets will
equally instruct you to admire[2] the ancients.'

Crites had no sooner left speaking, but Eugenius,
5 who had[3] waited with some impatience for it, thus
began :

'I have observed in your speech, that the former
part of it is convincing as to what the moderns have
profited by the rules of the ancients ; but in the latter
10 you are careful to conceal how much they have excelled them ; we own all the helps we have from them,
and want neither veneration nor gratitude, while we
acknowledge that, to overcome them, we must make
use of the advantages we have received from them :
15 but to these assistances we have joined our own in-
dustry ; for, had we sat down with a dull imitation of
them, we might then have lost somewhat of the old
perfection, but never acquired any that was new. We
draw not therefore after their lines, but those of nature ;
20 and having the life before us, besides the experience
of all they knew, it is no wonder if we hit some airs
and features which they have missed. I deny not
what you urge of arts and sciences, that they have
flourished in some ages more than others ; but your
25 instance in philosophy makes for me : for if natural
causes be more known now than in the time of
Aristotle, because more studied, it follows that poesy
and other arts may, with the same pains, arrive still
nearer to perfection ; and, that granted, it will rest
30 for you to prove that they wrought more perfect
images of human life than we ; which seeing in

---

[1] good ones, A.   [2] esteem, A.   [3] A *om.* had.

your discourse you have avoided to make good, it
shall now be my task to show you some part of their
defects, and some few excellencies of the moderns.
And I think there is none among us can imagine
I do it enviously, or with purpose to detract from 5
them; for what interest of fame or profit can the
living lose by the reputation of the dead? On the
other side, it is a great truth which Velleius Paterculus affirms[n]: *Audita visis libentius laudamus; et
præsentia invidia, præterita admiratione prosequimur;* 10
et his nos obrui, illis instrui credimus: that praise or
censure is certainly the most sincere, which unbribed
posterity shall give us.

'Be pleased then in the first place to take notice,
that the Greek poesy, which Crites has affirmed to 15
have arrived to perfection in the reign of the old
comedy, was so far from it, that the distinction of
it into acts was not known to them; or if it were,
it is yet so darkly delivered to us that we cannot
make it out. 20

'All we know of it is, from the singing of their
Chorus; and that too is so uncertain, that in some
of their plays we have reason to conjecture they sung
more than five times. Aristotle indeed divides the
integral parts of a play into four. First, the *Protasis*, 25
or entrance, which gives light only to the characters
of the persons, and proceeds very little into any part
of the action. Secondly, the *Epitasis*, or working up
of the plot; where the play grows warmer, the design
or action of it is drawing on, and you see something 30
promising that it will come to pass. Thirdly, the
Catastasis, called by the Romans, *Status*, the height

and full growth of the play: we may call it properly
the counter-turn[1], which destroys that expectation,
imbroils the action in new difficulties, and leaves you
far distant from that hope in which it found you ; as
5 you may have observed in a violent stream resisted
by a narrow passage,—it runs round to an eddy, and
carries back the waters with more swiftness than it
brought them on.   Lastly, the *Catastrophe,* which the
Grecians called λύσις, the French *le denouement,* and
10 we the discovery, or unravelling of the plot: there
you see all things settling again upon their first foundations ; and, the obstacles which hindered the design
or action of the play once removed, it ends with that
resemblance of truth and nature, that the audience
15 are satisfied with the conduct of it.   Thus this great
man delivered to us the image of a play ; and I must
confess it is so lively, that from thence much light has
been derived to the forming it more perfectly into acts
and scenes : but what poet first limited to five the
20 number of the acts, I know not; only we see it so
firmly established in the time of Horace, that he gives
it for a rule in comedy,—*Neu brevior quinto, neu sit
productior actu.*[n]   So that you see the Grecians cannot
be said to have consummated this art ; writing rather
25 by entrances, than by acts, and having rather a general
indigested notion of a play, than knowing how and
where to bestow the particular graces of it.

'But since the Spaniards at this day allow but three
acts, which they call *Jornadas*[n], to a play, and the
30 Italians in many of theirs follow them, when I condemn the ancients, I declare it is not altogether

[1] A has, 'Thirdly the Catastasis or Counterturn': the rest *om.*

because they have not five acts to every play, but
because they have not confined themselves to one
certain number : it is building an house without a
model ; and when they succeeded in such undertakings,
they ought to have sacrificed to Fortune, not to 5
the Muses.

'Next, for the plot, which Aristotle called τὸ μυθὸς [n],
and often τῶν πραγμάτων σύνθεσις, and from him the
Romans *Fabula* ; it has already been judiciously observed by a late writer, that in their tragedies it was 10
only some tale derived from Thebes or Troy, or at
least something that happened in those two ages ;
which was worn so threadbare by the pens of all the
epic poets, and even by tradition itself of the talkative Greeklings, (as Ben Johnson calls them,) that 15
before it came upon the stage, it was already known
to all the audience : and the people, so soon as ever
they heard the name of Oedipus, knew as well as the
poet, that he had killed his father by a mistake, and
committed incest with his mother, before the play ; 20
that they were now to hear of a great plague, an
oracle, and the ghost of Laius : so that they sat with
a yawning kind of expectation, till he was to come
with his eyes pulled out, and speak a hundred or
more[1] verses in a tragic tone, in complaint of his 25
misfortunes. But one Oedipus, Hercules, or Medea,
had been tolerable : poor people, they escaped not so
good cheap [n] ; they had still the *chapon bouillé* set
before them, till their appetites were cloyed with the
same dish, and, the novelty being gone, the pleasure 30
vanished ; so that one main end of Dramatic Poesy

---

[1] hundred or two of, A.

in its definition, which was to cause delight, was of consequence destroyed.

'In their comedies, the Romans generally borrowed their plots from the Greek poets; and theirs was
5 commonly a little girl stolen or wandered from her parents, brought back unknown to the city[1], there [falling into the hands of] some young fellow, who, by the help of his servant, cheats his father; and when her time comes, to cry,—*Juno Lucina, fer*
10 *opem,*—one or other sees a little box or cabinet which was carried away with her, and so discovers her to her friends, if some god do not prevent it, by coming down in a machine, and taking[2] the thanks of it to himself.

15 'By the plot you may guess much of the characters of the persons. An old father, who would willingly, before he dies, see his son well married; his debauched son, kind in his nature to his mistress[3], but miserably in want of money; a servant or slave, who
20 has so much wit to strike in with him, and help to dupe his father; a braggadocio captain, a parasite, and a lady of pleasure.

'As for the poor honest maid, on whom the story is built, and who ought to be one of the principal
25 actors in the play, she is commonly a mute in it: she has the breeding of the old Elizabeth way, which was[4] for maids to be seen and not to be heard; and it is enough you know she is willing to be married, when the fifth act requires it.

30 'These are plots built after the Italian mode of

[1] the same city, A.
[2] *take*, A.
[3] so C; Mistres, B; Wench, A.
[4] A *om.* which was.

houses,—you see through them all at once: the characters are indeed the imitation of nature, but so narrow, as if they had imitated only an eye or an hand, and did not dare to venture on the lines of a face, or the proportion of a body. 5

'But in how strait a compass soever they have bounded their plots and characters, we will pass it by, if they have regularly pursued them, and perfectly observed those three unities of time, place, and action; the knowledge of which you say is derived 10 to us from them. But in the first place give me leave to tell you, that the unity of place, however it might be practised by them, was never any of their rules: we neither find it in Aristotle, Horace, or any who have written of it, till in our age the French poets 15 first made it a precept of the stage. The unity of time, even Terence himself, who was the best and most regular of them, has neglected: his *Heauton-timorumenos*, or Self-Punisher, takes up visibly two days, says Scaliger; the two first acts concluding 20 the first day, the three last the day ensuing[1]; and Euripides, in tying himself to one day, has committed an absurdity never to be forgiven him; for in one of his tragedies[n] he has made Theseus go from Athens to Thebes, which was about forty English 25 miles, under the walls of it to give battle, and appear victorious in the next act; and yet, from the time of his departure to the return of the Nuntius, who gives the relation of his victory, Æthra and the

---

[1] A has, 'therefore, sayes Scaliger, the two first acts concluding the first day were acted overnight; the three last on the ensuing day.'

Chorus have but thirty-six verses; which[1] is not
for every mile a verse.

   'The like error is as evident in Terence his *Eunuch*,
when Laches, the old man, enters by mistake into
5 the house[2] of Thais; where, betwixt his exit and
the entrance of Pythias, who comes to give ample
relation of the disorders[3] he has raised within, Parmeno, who was left upon the stage, has not above
five lines to speak. *C'est bien employer[4] un temps si*
10 *court*, says the French poet, who furnished me with
one of the observations: and almost all their tragedies
will afford us examples of the like nature.

   'It is true[5], they have kept the continuity, or, as
you called it, *liaison des scenes*, somewhat better:
15 two do not perpetually come in together, talk, and
go out together; and other two succeed them, and
do the same throughout the act, which the English
call by the name of single scenes; but the reason
is, because they have seldom above two or three
20 scenes, properly so called, in every act; for it is to
be accounted a new scene, not only every time[6] the
stage is empty; but every person who enters, though
to others, makes it so; because he introduces a new
business. Now the plots of their plays being narrow,
25 and the persons few, one of their acts was written
in a less compass than one of our well-wrought
scenes; and yet they are often deficient even in
this. To go no further than Terence; you find in
the *Eunuch*, Antipho entering single in the midst

[1] that, A.   [2] in a mistake the house, A.
[3] Garboyles, A.   [4] employé, A.
[5] 'Tis true, A.   [6] not every time, A.

of the third act, after Chremes and Pythias were
gone off; in the same play you have likewise Dorias
beginning the fourth act alone; and after she had
made a relation of what was done at the Soldier's[1]
entertainment, (which by the way was very inarti- 5
ficial, because she was presumed to speak directly
to the audience, and to acquaint them with what was
necessary to be known, but yet should have been so
contrived by the poet as to have been told by persons
of the drama to one another, and so by them to have 10
come to the knowledge of the people,) she quits the
stage, and Phædria enters next, alone likewise: he
also gives you an account of himself, and of his
returning from the country, in monologue; to which
unnatural way of narration Terence is subject in 15
all his plays. In his *Adelphi*, or Brothers, Syrus
and Demea enter after the scene was broken by
the departure of Sostrata, Geta, and Canthara; and
indeed you can scarce look into any of his comedies,
where you will not presently discover the same in- 20
terruption.

'But as they have failed both in laying of their
plots, and in the management[2], swerving from the
rules of their own art by misrepresenting nature to
us, in which they have ill satisfied one intention of 25
a play, which was delight; so in the instructive part
they have erred worse: instead of punishing vice
and rewarding virtue, they have often shewn a pros-
perous wickedness, and an unhappy piety: they have
set before us a bloody image of revenge in Medea, 30
and given her dragons to convey her safe from punish-

---

[1] Souldiers, A.   [2] managing of 'em, A.

ment; a Priam and Astyanax murdered, and Cassandra ravished, and the lust and murder ending
in the victory of him who acted them: in short,
there is no indecorum in any of our modern plays,
5 which if I would excuse, I could not shadow with
some authority from the ancients.

'And one farther note of them let me leave you:
tragedies and comedies were not writ then as they
are now, promiscuously, by the same person; but
10 he who found his genius bending to the one, never
attempted the other way.　This is so plain, that I
need not instance to you, that Aristophanes, Plautus,
Terence, never any of them writ a tragedy; Æschylus,
Euripides[n], Sophocles, and Seneca, never meddled
15 with comedy: the sock and buskin were not worn
by the same poet.　Having then so much care to
excel in one kind, very little is to be pardoned them,
if they miscarried in it; and this would lead me to
the consideration of their wit, had not Crites given
20 me sufficient warning not to be too bold in my judgment of it; because, the languages being dead, and
many of the customs and little accidents on which
it depended lost to us, we are not competent judges
of it.　But though I grant that here and there we
25 may miss the application of a proverb or a custom,
yet a thing well said will be wit in all languages;
and though it may lose something in the translation,
yet to him who reads it in the original, 'tis still the
same: he has an idea of its excellency, though it
30 cannot pass from his mind into any other expression
or words than those in which he finds it.　When
Phædria, in the *Eunuch*, had a command from his

mistress to be absent two days, and, encouraging himself to go through with it, said, *Tandem ego non illa caream, si sit opus*[1], *vel totum triduum?*—Parmeno, to mock the softness of his master, lifting up his hands and eyes, cries out, as it were in admira- 5 tion, *Hui! universum triduum!* [n] the elegancy of which *universum*, though it cannot be rendered in our language, yet leaves an impression on our souls: but this happens seldom in him; in Plautus oftener, who is infinitely too bold in his metaphors and coin- 10 ing words, out of which many times his wit is nothing; which questionless was one reason why Horace falls upon him so severely in those verses:

> *Sed proavi nostri Plautinos et numeros et*
> *Laudavere sales, nimium patienter utrumque,* 15
> *Ne dicam stolidè* [n].

For Horace himself was cautious to obtrude a new word on his readers, and makes custom and common use the best measure of receiving it into our writings: 20

> *Multa renascentur quæ nunc [jam] cecidere, cadentque*
> *Quæ nunc sunt in honore vocabula, si volet usus,*
> *Quem penes arbitrium est, et jus, et norma loquendi* [n].

The not observing this rule is that which the world has blamed in our satyrist, Cleveland[2]: to 25 express a thing hard and unnaturally, is his new way of elocution. 'Tis true, no poet but may sometimes use a catachresis [n]: Virgil does it—

> *Mistaque ridenti colocasia fundet acantho—* [n]

[1] si opus sit, A.   [2] so A; Cleiveland, B.

in his eclogue of Pollio; and in his seventh Æneid,

mirantur et undæ,
Miratur nemus insuetum fulgentia longe
Scuta virum fluvio pictasque innare carinas.

5 And Ovid once so modestly, that he asks leave to
do it:

——————— *quem, si verbo audacia detur,*
Haud metuam summi dixisse Palatia cæli [n].

calling the court of Jupiter by the name of Augustus
10 his palace; though in another place he is more bold,
where he says,—*et longas visent Capitolia pompas.*
But to do this always, and never be able to write
a line without it, though it may be admired by some
few pedants, will not pass upon those who know that
15 wit is best conveyed to us in the most easy language;
and is most to be admired when a great thought
comes dressed in words so commonly received, that
it is understood by the meanest apprehensions, as
the best meat is the most easily digested: but we
20 cannot read a verse of Cleiveland's without making
a face at it, as if every word were a pill to
swallow: he gives us many times a hard nut to
break our teeth, without a kernel for our pains. So
that there is this difference betwixt his Satires and
25 doctor Donne's; that the one gives us deep thoughts
in common language, though rough cadence; the
other gives us common thoughts in abstruse words:
'tis true, in some places his wit is independent of his
words, as in that of the rebel Scot:

30   Had Cain been Scot, God would have chang'd his doom;
     Not forc'd him wander, but confin'd him home [n].

Si sic omnia dixisset! [n] This is wit in all languages : it is like Mercury, never to be lost or killed :—and so that other—

> For beauty, like white powder, makes no noise,
> And yet the silent hypocrite destroys. 5

You see, the last line is highly metaphorical, but it is so soft and gentle, that it does not shock us as we read it.

'But, to return from whence I have digressed, to the consideration of the ancients' writing, and their 10 wit; (of which by this time you will grant us in some measure to be fit judges.) Though I see many excellent thoughts in Seneca, yet he of them who had a genius most proper for the stage, was Ovid; he had a way of writing so fit to stir up a pleasing 15 admiration and concernment, which are the objects of a tragedy, and to shew the various movements of a soul combating betwixt two different passions, that, had he lived in our age, or in his own could have writ with our advantages, no man but must have 20 yielded to him; and therefore I am confident the *Medea* [n] is none of his : for, though I esteem it for the gravity and sententiousness of it, which he himself concludes to be suitable to a tragedy,—*Omne genus scripti gravitate tragœdia vincit* [n],—yet it moves 25 not my soul enough to judge that he, who in the epick way wrote things so near the drama as the story of Myrrha, of Caunus and Biblis, and the rest, should stir up no more concernment where he most endeavoured it [n]. The master-piece of Seneca I hold 30 to be that scene in the *Troades*, where Ulysses is seeking for Astyanax to kill him : there you see the

tenderness of a mother so represented in Andromache, that it raises compassion to a high degree in the reader, and bears the nearest resemblance of any thing in the tragedies of the ancients [1] to the excellent
5 scenes of passion in Shakspeare, or in Fletcher: for love-scenes, you will find few among them; their tragick poets dealt not with that soft passion, but with lust, cruelty, revenge, ambition, and those bloody actions they produced; which were more capable
10 of raising horrour than compassion in an audience: leaving love untouched, whose gentleness would have tempered them; which is the most frequent of all the passions, and which, being the private concernment of every person, is soothed by viewing its own image
15 in a publick entertainment.

'Among their comedies, we find a scene or two of tenderness, and that where you would least expect it, in Plautus; but to speak generally, their lovers say little, when they see each other, but *anima mea, vita*
20 *mea*; Ζωὴ καὶ ψυχῆ [n], as the women in Juvenal's time used to cry out in the fury of their kindness [2]. Any sudden gust of passion (as an extasy of love in an unexpected meeting) cannot better be expressed than in a word and a sigh, breaking one another. Nature
25 is dumb on such occasions; and to make her speak, would be to represent her unlike herself. But there are a thousand other concernments of lovers, as jealousies, complaints, contrivances, and the like, where not to open their minds at large to each other,
30 were to be wanting to their own love, and to the ex-

---

[1] their tragedies, A.
[2] kindness: then indeed to speak sense were an offence, A.

pectation of the audience ; who watch the movements
of their minds, as much as the changes of their fortunes. For the imaging of the first is properly the work
of a poet ; the latter he borrows from [1] the historian.'

Eugenius was proceeding in that part of his dis- 5
course, when Crites interrupted him. 'I see,' said
he, 'Eugenius and I are never like to have this
question decided betwixt us ; for he maintains, the
moderns have acquired a new perfection in writing ;
I can only grant they have altered the mode of it. 10
Homer described his heroes men of great appetites,
lovers of beef broiled upon the coals, and good
fellows ; contrary to the practice of the French
Romances, whose heroes neither eat, nor drink, nor
sleep, for love. Virgil makes Æneas a bold avower 15
of his own virtues :

Sum pius Æneas, fama super æthera notus [n] ;

which, in the civility of our poets is the character of
a fanfaron or Hector : for with us the knight takes
occasion to walk out, or sleep, to avoid the vanity of 20
telling his own story, which the trusty 'squire is ever
to perform for him. So in their love-scenes, of
which Eugenius spoke last, the ancients were more
hearty, we more talkative : they writ love as it was
then the mode to make it ; and I will grant thus much 25
to Eugenius, that perhaps one of their poets, had he
lived in our age, *si foret hoc nostrum fato delapsus in
ævum* [n], (as Horace says of Lucilius,) he had altered
many things ; not that they were not natural [2] before,
but that he might accommodate himself to the age in 30
which he lived [3]. Yet in the mean time, we are not to

---

[1] of, A.   [2] as natural, A.   [3] age he liv'd in, A.

conclude any thing rashly against those great men, but preserve to them the dignity of masters, and give that honour to their memories, *quos Libitina sacravit,* part of which we expect may be paid to us in future times.'

This moderation of Crites, as it was pleasing to all the company, so it put an end to that dispute ; which Eugenius, who seemed to have the better of the argument, would urge no farther : but Lisideius, after he had acknowledged himself of Eugenius his opinion concerning the ancients, yet told him, he had forborne, till his discourse were ended, to ask him why he preferred the English plays above those of other nations ? and whether we ought not to submit our stage to the exactness of our next neighbours ?

'Though,' said Eugenius, 'I am at all times ready to defend the honour of my country against the French, and to maintain, we are as well able to vanquish them with our pens, as our ancestors have been with their swords ; yet, if you please,' added he, looking upon Neander, 'I will commit this cause to my friend's management ; his opinion of our plays is the same with mine : and besides, there is no reason, that Crites and I, who have now left the stage, should re-enter so suddenly upon it ; which is against the laws of comedy.'

'If the question had been stated,' replied Lisideius, 'who had writ best, the French or English, forty years ago, I should have been of your opinion, and adjudged the honour to our own nation ; but since that time,' (said he, turning towards Neander,) 'we have been so long together bad Englishmen, that we had not leisure to be good poets. Beaumont, Fletcher, and Johnson, (who were only capable of bringing us to that degree of perfection which we have,) were just then leaving the world ; as if in an age of so much horrour, wit, and those milder studies of humanity, had no farther business among us. But the Muses, who ever follow peace, went to plant in another country : it was then, that the great Cardinal of Richelieu began to take them into his protection ; and that, by his encouragement, Corneille[n], and some other Frenchmen, reformed their theatre, (which before was as much below ours, as it now surpasses it and the rest of Europe). But because Crites in his discourse for the ancients has prevented me, by observing[1] many rules of the stage which the moderns have borrowed from them, I shall only, in short, demand of you, whether you are not convinced that of all nations the French have best observed them ? In the unity of time you find them so scrupulous, that it yet remains a dispute among their poets, whether the artificial day of twelve hours, more or less, be not meant by Aristotle, rather than the natural one of twenty-four ; and consequently, whether all plays ought not to be reduced into that compass. This I can testify, that in all their dramas writ within these last twenty years and upwards, I have not observed any that have extended the time to thirty hours : in the unity of place they are full as scrupulous ; for many of their criticks limit it to that very spot of ground where the play is supposed to begin ; none of them exceed the compass of the same town

---

[1] touching upon, A.

or city. The unity of action in all plays is yet more
conspicuous; for they do not burden them with under-
plots, as the English do : which is the reason why
many scenes of our tragi-comedies carry on a design
5 that is nothing of kin to the main plot ; and that we
see two distinct webs in a play, like those in ill-
wrought stuffs ; and two actions, that is, two plays,
carried on together, to the confounding of the
audience ; who, before they are warm in their con-
10 cernments for one part, are diverted to another ; and
by that means espouse the interest of neither. From
hence likewise it arises, that the one half of our actors
are not known to the other. They keep their dis-
tances, as if they were Mountagues and Capulets, and
15 seldom begin an acquaintance till the last scene of the
fifth act, when they are all to meet upon the stage.
There is no theatre in the world has any thing so
absurd as the English tragi-comedy ; 'tis a drama of
our own invention, and the fashion of it is enough to
20 proclaim it so ; here a course of mirth, there another
of sadness and passion, and a third of honour and a
duel[1] : thus, in two hours and a half, we run through
all the fits of Bedlam. The French affords you as
much variety on the same day, but they do it not so
25 unseasonably, or *mal à propos*, as we : our poets present you the play and the farce together ; and our
stages still retain somewhat of the original civility of
the Red Bull [n] :

Atque ursum et pugiles media inter carmina poscunt [n].

30 The end of tragedies or serious plays, says Aristotle,
is to beget admiration, compassion, or concernment ;

_____
[1] a third of Honour, and fourth a Duel, A.

but are not mirth and compassion things incompatible?
and is it not evident that the poet must of necessity
destroy the former by intermingling of the latter?
that is, he must ruin the sole end and object of his
tragedy, to introduce somewhat that is forced into it[1], 5
and is not of the body of it. Would you not think
that physician mad, who, having prescribed a purge,
should immediately order you to take restringents[2]?

'But to leave our plays, and return to theirs. I
have noted one great advantage they have had in the 10
plotting of their tragedies; that is, they are always
grounded upon some known history: according to
that of Horace, *Ex noto fictum carmen sequar*[n]; and
in that they have so imitated the ancients, that they
have surpassed them. For the ancients, as was ob- 15
served before, took for the foundation of their plays
some poetical fiction, such as under that consideration
could move but little concernment in the audience,
because they already knew the event of it. But the
French goes farther: 20

> *Atque ita mentitur, sic veris falsa remiscet,*
> *Primo ne medium, medio ne discrepet imum*[n].

He so interweaves truth with probable fiction, that
he puts a pleasing fallacy upon us; mends the intrigues of fate, and dispenses with the severity of 25
history, to reward that virtue which has been rendered to us there unfortunate. Sometimes the story
has left the success[n] so doubtful, that the writer is
free, by the privilege of a poet, to take that which of
two or more relations will best suit with his design: 30
as for example, in[3] the death of Cyrus, whom Justin

---

[1] forced in, A.   [2] restringents upon it, A.   [3] A *om.*

and some others report to have perished in the Scythian war, but Xenophon affirms to have died in his bed of extreme old age [n]. Nay more, when the event is past dispute, even then we are willing to be de-
5 ceived, and the poet, if he contrives it with appearance of truth, has all the audience of his party; at least during the time his play is acting: so naturally we are kind to virtue, when our own interest is not in question, that we take it up as the general concernment
10 of mankind. On the other side, if you consider the historical plays of Shakspeare, they are rather so many chronicles of kings, or the business many times of thirty or forty years, cramped into a representation of two hours and an half; which is not to imitate or
15 paint nature, but rather to draw her in miniature, to take her in little; to look upon her through the wrong end of a perspective, and receive her images not only much less, but infinitely more imperfect than the life: this, instead of making a play delightful, renders it
20 ridiculous :—

Quodcunque ostendis mihi sic, incredulus odi [u].

For the spirit of man cannot be satisfied but with truth, or at least verisimility; and a poem is to contain, if not τὰ ἔτυμα, yet ἐτύμοισιν ὁμοῖα, as one of the
25 Greek poets has expressed it [n].

'Another thing in which the French differ from us and from the Spaniards, is, that they do not embarrass, or cumber themselves with too much plot; they only represent so much of a story as will constitute one
30 whole and great action sufficient for a play; we, who undertake more, do but multiply adventures; which,

not being produced from one another, as effects from causes, but barely following, constitute many actions in the drama, and consequently make it many plays.

'But by pursuing closely[1] one argument, which is not cloyed with many turns, the French have gained 5 more liberty for verse, in which they write ; they have leisure to dwell on a subject which deserves it ; and to represent the passions, (which we have acknow-ledged to be the poet's work,) without being hurried from one thing to another, as we are in the plays 10 of Calderon, which we have seen lately upon our theatres, under the name of Spanish plots. I have taken notice but of one tragedy of ours, whose plot has that uniformity and unity of design in it, which I have commended in the French ; and that is *Rollo*[n], 15 or rather, under the name of Rollo, the Story of Bassianus and Geta in Herodian : there indeed the plot is neither large nor intricate, but just enough to fill the minds of the audience, not to cloy them. Besides, you see it founded upon the truth of history, 20 —only the time of the action is not reduceable to the strictness of the rules ; and you see in some places a little farce mingled, which is below the dignity of the other parts ; and in this all our poets are extremely peccant : even Ben Johnson himself, in *Sejanus* and 25 *Catiline*, has given us this oleo[n] of a play, this un-natural mixture of comedy and tragedy ; which to me sounds just as ridiculously as the history of David with the merry humours of Golia's[2]. In *Sejanus* you may take notice of the scene betwixt Livia and the 30 physician, which is a pleasant satire upon the artificial

---

[1] close, A.   [2] Goliah's, C.

helps of beauty: in *Catiline* you may see the parliament of women; the little envies of them to one
another; and all that passes betwixt Curio and Fulvia:
scenes admirable in their kind, but of an ill mingle
5 with the rest.

'But I return again to the French writers, who, as
I have said, do not burden themselves too much with
plot, which has been reproached to them by an ingenious person of our nation as a fault; for, he says,
10 they commonly make but one person considerable in
a play; they dwell on him, and his concernments,
while the rest of the persons are only subservient to
set him off. If he intends this by it,—that there is
one person in the play who is of greater dignity than
15 the rest, he must tax, not only theirs, but those of the
ancients, and which he would be loth to do, the best
of ours; for it is impossible but that one person must
be more conspicuous in it than any other, and consequently the greatest share in the action must devolve
20 on him. We see it so in the management of all
affairs; even in the most equal aristocracy, the balance
cannot be so justly poised, but some one will be
superiour to the rest, either in parts, fortune, interest,
or the consideration of some glorious exploit; which
25 will reduce the greatest part of business into his
hands.

'But, if he would have us to imagine, that in
exalting one character the rest of them are neglected,
and that all of them have not some share or other in
30 the action of the play, I desire him to produce any of
Corneille's tragedies, wherein every person, like so
many servants in a well-governed family, has not some

employment, and who is not necessary to the carrying on of the plot, or at least to your understanding it.

'There are indeed some protatick[n] persons in the ancients, whom they make use of in their plays, either to hear or give the relation: but the French avoid 5 this with great address, making their narrations only to, or by such, who are some way interessed in the main design. And now I am speaking of relations, I cannot take a fitter opportunity to add this in favour of the French, that they often use them with better 10 judgment and more *à propos* than the English do. Not that I commend narrations in general,—but there are two sorts of them. One, of those things which are antecedent to the play, and are related to make the conduct of it more clear to us. But 'tis a fault to 15 choose such subjects for the stage as will force us on that rock, because we see they are seldom listened to by the audience, and that is many times the ruin of the play; for, being once let pass without attention, the audience can never recover themselves to under- 20 stand the plot: and indeed it is somewhat unreasonable that they should be put to so much trouble, as that, to comprehend what passes in their sight, they must have recourse to what was done, perhaps, ten or twenty years ago. 25

'But there is another sort of relations, that is, of things happening in the action of the play, and sup- posed to be done behind the scenes; and this is many times both convenient and beautiful; for by it the French avoid the tumult to which we are subject[1] 30 in England, by representing duels, battles, and the

---

[1] which we are subject to, A.

like; which renders our stage too like the theatres where they fight prizes. For what is more ridiculous than to represent an army with a drum and five men behind it; all which the hero of the other side is 5 to drive in before him; or to see a duel fought, and one slain with two or three thrusts of the foils, which we know are so blunted, that we might give a man an hour to kill another in good earnest with them.

'I have observed that in all our tragedies, the 10 audience cannot forbear laughing when the actors are to die; it is the most comick part of the whole play. All *passions* may be lively represented on the stage, if to the well-writing of them the actor supplies a good commanded voice, and limbs that move easily, and 15 without stiffness; but there are many *actions* which can never be imitated to a just height: dying especially is a thing which none but a Roman gladiator could naturally perform on the stage, when he did not imitate or represent, but do it[1]; and therefore it is 20 better to omit the representation of it.

'The words of a good writer, which describe it lively, will make a deeper impression of belief in us than all the actor can insinuate into us[2], when he seems to fall dead before us; as a poet in the descrip- 25 tion of a beautiful garden, or a meadow, will please our imagination more than the place itself can please our sight. When we see death represented, we are convinced it is but fiction; but when we hear it related, our eyes, the strongest witnesses, are wanting, which 30 might have undeceived us; and we are all willing to favour the sleight, when the poet does not too grossly

---

[1] naturally do it, A.　　　　　[2] perswade us to, A.

impose on us.   They therefore who imagine these relations would make no concernment in the audience, are deceived, by confounding them with the other, which are of things antecedent to the play : those are made often in cold blood, as I may say, to the audience ; 5 but these are warmed with our concernments, which were before awakened in the play.   What the philo-sophers say of motion, that, when it is once begun, it continues of itself, and will do so to eternity, without some stop put to it, is clearly true on this occasion : 10 the soul, being already moved with the characters and fortunes of those imaginary persons, continues going of its own accord ; and we are no more weary to hear what becomes of them when they are not on the stage, than we are to listen to the news of an absent mistress. 15 But it is objected, that if one part of the play may be related, then why not all ?   I answer, some parts of the action are more fit to be represented, some to be related.   Corneille says judiciously, that the poet is not obliged to expose to view all particular actions 20 which conduce to the principal : he ought to select such of them to be seen, which will appear with the greatest beauty, either by the magnificence of the show, or the vehemence of passions which they pro-duce, or some other charm which they have in them ; 25 and let the rest arrive to the audience by narration. 'Tis a great mistake in us to believe the French present no part of the action on the stage ; every alteration or crossing of a design, every new-sprung passion, and turn of it, is a part of the action, and 30 much the noblest, except we conceive nothing to be action till the players come[1] to blows ; as if the painting

---

[1] they come, A

E

of the hero's mind were not more properly the poet's
work than the strength of his body.   Nor does this
anything contradict the opinion of Horace, where he
tells us,

5
Segnius irritant animos demissa per aurem,
Quam quæ sunt oculis subjecta fidelibus.

For he says immediately after,

——— —————————*Non tamen intus*
Digna geri promes in scenam ; multaq; *tolles*
10
Ex oculis, quæ mox narret facundia præsens.

Among which many he recounts some :

Nec pueros coram populo Medea trucidet,
Aut in avem Progne mutetur, Cadmus in anguem [n] *; &c.*

That is, those actions which by reason of their cruelty
15 will cause aversion in us, or by reason of their im-
possibility, unbelief, ought either wholly to be avoided
by a poet, or only delivered by narration.   To which
we may have leave to add, such as, to avoid tumult,
(as was before hinted,) or to reduce the plot into
20 a more reasonable compass of time, or for defect of
beauty in them, are rather to be related than presented
to the eye.   Examples of all these kinds are frequent,
not only among all the ancients, but in the best received of our English poets.   We find Ben Johnson
25 using them in his *Magnetick Lady* [n], where one comes
out from dinner, and relates the quarrels and disorders of it, to save the undecent appearance of them
on the stage, and to abbreviate the story; and this
in express imitation of Terence, who had done the

same before him in his *Eunuch*, where Pythias makes
the like relation of what had happened within at the
Soldiers[1] entertainment. The relations likewise of
Sejanus's death, and the prodigies before it, are
remarkable ; the one of which was hid from sight, 5
to avoid the horrour and tumult of the representation ; the other, to shun the introducing of things
impossible to be believed. In that excellent play,
The King and no King[n], Fletcher goes yet farther ;
for the whole unravelling of the plot is done by 10
narration in the fifth act, after the manner of the
ancients ; and it moves great concernment in the
audience, though it be only a relation of what was
done many years before the play. I could multiply
other instances, but these are sufficient to prove that 15
there is no errour in choosing a subject which requires this sort of narrations ; in the ill management[2]
of them, there may.

'But I find I have been too long in this discourse,
since the French have many other excellencies not 20
common to us ; as that you never see any of their
plays end with a conversion, or simple change of
will, which is the ordinary way which our poets
use to end theirs. It shews little art in the conclusion of a dramatick poem, when they who have 25
hindered the felicity during the four acts, desist from
it in the fifth, without some powerful cause to take
them off their design[3] ; and though I deny not but
such reasons may be found, yet it is a path that is
cautiously to be trod, and the poet is to be sure he 30
convinces the audience that the motive is strong

---

[1] Souldiers, A.   [2] managing, A   [3] A *om.* their design.

enough. As for example, the conversion of the Usurer in *The Scornful Lady*[n], seems to me a little forced; for, being an Usurer, which implies a lover of money to the highest degree of covetousness,—
5 and such the poet has represented him,—the account he gives for the sudden change is, that he has been duped by the wild young fellow; which in reason might render him more wary another time, and make him punish himself with harder fare and coarser
10 clothes, to get up again what he had lost[1]: but that he should look on it as a judgment, and so repent, we may expect to hear[2] in a sermon, but I should never endure it in a play.

'I pass by this; neither will I insist on the care
15 they take, that no person after his first entrance shall ever appear, but the business which brings him upon the stage shall be evident; which rule[3], if observed, must needs render all the events in the play more natural; for there you see the probability of every
20 accident, in the cause that produced it; and that which appears chance in the play, will seem so reasonable to you, that you will there find it almost necessary: so that in the exit of the actor[4] you have a clear account of his[5] purpose and design in the next
25 entrance; (though, if the scene be well wrought, the event will commonly deceive you;) for there is nothing so absurd, says Corneille, as for an actor to leave the stage, only because he has no more to say.

'I should now speak of the beauty of their rhyme,
30 and the just reason I have to prefer that way of

---

[1] to get it up again, A.   [2] hear of, A.   [3] A *om.* rule.
[4] exits of the Actors, A.   [5] their, A.

writing in tragedies before ours in blank verse ; but
because it is partly received by us, and therefore not
altogether peculiar to them, I will say no more of it
in relation to their plays. For our own, I doubt not
but it will exceedingly beautify them ; and I can see 5
but one reason why it should not generally obtain,
that is, because our poets write so ill in it. This
indeed may prove a more prevailing argument than
all others which are used to destroy it, and therefore
I am only troubled when great and judicious poets, 10
and those who are acknowledged such, have writ
or spoke against it : as for others, they are to be answered by that one sentence of an ancient author :—
Sed ut primo ad consequendos eos quos priores ducimus,
accendimur, ita ubi aut præteriri, aut æquari eos posse 15
desperavimus, studium cum spe senescit : quod, scilicet,
assequi non potest, sequi desinit ; . . . præteritoque eo in
quo eminere non possumus, aliquid in quo nitamur,
conquirimus [n].'

Lisideius concluded in this manner ; and Neander, 20
after a little pause, thus answered him :

'I shall grant Lisideius, without much dispute,
a great part of what he has urged against us ; for
I acknowledge that the French contrive their plots
more regularly, and observe the laws of comedy, and 25
decorum of the stage, (to speak generally,) with more
exactness than the English. Farther, I deny not
but he has taxed us justly in some irregularities of
ours, which he has mentioned ; yet, after all, I am
of opinion that neither our faults nor their virtues 30
are considerable enough to place them above us.

'For the lively imitation of nature being in the

definition of a play, those which best fulfil that law
ought to be esteemed superior to the others. 'Tis
true, those beauties of the French poesy are such
as will raise perfection higher where it is, but are
5 not sufficient to give it where it is not: they are
indeed the beauties of a statue, but not of a man,
because not animated with the soul of poesy, which
is imitation of humour and passions: and this Lisideius himself, or any other, however biassed to their
10 party, cannot but acknowledge, if he will either compare the humours of our comedies, or the characters
of our serious plays, with theirs. He who [1] will look
upon theirs which have been written till these last
ten years, or thereabouts, will find it an hard matter
15 to pick out two or three passable humours amongst
them. Corneille himself, their arch-poet, what has
he produced except *The Liar* [n], and you know how
it was cried up in France; but when it came upon
the English stage, though well translated, and that
20 part of Dorant acted to so much advantage [2] as I am
confident it never received in its own country, the
most favourable to it would not put it [3] in competition
with many of Fletcher's or Ben Johnson's [n]. In the
rest of Corneille's comedies you have little humour;
25 he tells you himself, his way is, first to shew two
lovers in good intelligence with each other; in the
working up of the play to embroil them by some
mistake, and in the latter end to clear it, and reconcile
them [4].

30　　'But of late years Moliere [5], the younger Corneille,

---

[1] He that, A.　　　[2] A adds 'by Mr. Hart.'　　　[3] A *om.* it.
[4] to clear it up, A.　　　[5] de Moliere, A.

Quinault, and some others, have been imitating afar off[1] the quick turns and graces of the English stage. They have mixed their serious plays with mirth, like our tragi-comedies, since the death of Cardinal Richelieu n; which Lisideius and many others not observing, have commended that in them for a virtue which they themselves no longer practise. Most of their new plays are, like some of ours, derived from the Spanish novels n. There is scarce one of them without a veil, and a trusty Diego, who drolls much after the rate of *The Adventures* n. But their humours, if I may grace them with that name, are so thin-sown, that never above one of them comes up in any play. I dare take upon me to find more variety of them in some one play of Ben Johnson's, than in all theirs together; as he who has seen *The Alchemist, The Silent Woman,* or *Bartholomew-Fair,* cannot but acknowledge with me.

'I grant the French have performed what was possible on the ground-work of the Spanish plays ; what was pleasant before, they have made regular : but there is not above one good play to be writ on ∙ all those plots ; they are too much alike to please often ; which we need not the experience of our own stage to justify. As for their new way of mingling mirth with serious plot, I do not, with Lisideius, condemn the thing, though I cannot approve their manner ˙ of doing it. He tells us, we cannot so speedily recollect ourselves after a scene of great passion and concernment, as to pass to another of mirth and humour, and to enjoy it with any relish : but why

[1] of afar off, A.

should he imagine the soul of man more heavy than his senses? Does not the eye pass from an unpleasant object to a pleasant in a much shorter time than is required to this? and does not the unpleasantness 5 of the first commend the beauty of the latter? The old rule of logick[n] might have convinced him, that contraries, when placed near, set off each other. A continued gravity keeps the spirit too much bent; we must refresh it sometimes, as we bait in a journey 10 that we may go on with greater ease. A scene of mirth, mixed with tragedy, has the same effect upon us which our musick has betwixt the acts; which we find[1] a relief to us from the best plots and language of the stage, if the discourses have been long. I 15 must therefore have stronger arguments, ere I am convinced that compassion and mirth in the same subject destroy each other; and in the mean time cannot but conclude, to the honour of our nation, that we have invented, increased, and perfected a more 20 pleasant way of writing for the stage, than was ever known to the ancients or moderns of any nation, which is tragi-comedy.

'And this leads me to wonder why Lisideius and many others should cry up the barrenness of the 25 French plots, above the variety and copiousness of the English. Their plots are single; they carry on one design, which is pushed forward by all the actors, every scene in the play contributing and moving towards it. Our plays[2], besides the main design, have 30 under-plots or by-concernments, of less considerable persons and intrigues, which are carried on with the

---

[1] and that we find, A.   [2] Ours, A.

motion of the main plot : as [1] they say the orb of the
fixed stars, and those of the planets, though they have
motions of their own, are whirled about by the motion
of the *primum mobile*, in which they are contained ".
That similitude expresses much of the English stage; 5
for if contrary motions may be found in nature to
agree ; if a planet can go east and west at the same
time ;—one way by virtue of his own motion, the
other by the force of the first mover ;—it will not be
difficult to imagine how the under-plot, which is only 10
different, not contrary to the great design, may naturally be conducted along with it.

'Eugenius has already shewn us, from the confes-
sion of the French poets, that the unity of action is
sufficiently preserved, if all the imperfect actions of 15
the play are conducing to the main design ; but when
those petty intrigues of a play are so ill ordered,
that they have no coherence with the other, I must
grant that Lisideius has reason to tax that want of
due connexion ; for co-ordination in a play is as dan- 20
gerous and unnatural as in a state. In the mean time
he must acknowledge, our variety, if well ordered,
will afford a greater pleasure to the audience.

'As for his other argument, that by pursuing one
single theme they gain an advantage to express and 25
work up the passions, I wish any example he could
bring from them would make it good; for I confess
their verses are to me the coldest I have ever read.
Neither, indeed, is it possible for them, in the way
they take, so to express passion, as that the effects 30
of it should appear in the concernment of an audience,

---

[1] just as, A.

their speeches being so many declamations, which
tire us with the length; so that instead of persuading
us to grieve for their imaginary heroes, we are concerned for our own trouble, as we are in tedious [1]
5 visits of bad company; we are in pain till they are
gone.   When the French stage came to be reformed
by Cardinal Richelieu, those long harangues were
introduced to comply with the gravity of a churchman.
Look upon the *Cinna* and the *Pompey*; they are not
10 so properly to be called plays, as long discourses of
reason of state; and *Polieucte* in matters of religion
is as solemn as the long stops upon our organs [u].
Since that time it is grown into a custom, and their
actors speak by the hour-glass, like our parsons [2];*
15 nay, they account it the grace of their parts, and
think themselves disparaged by the poet, if they may
not twice or thrice in a play entertain the audience
with a speech of an hundred lines [3].   I deny not but
this may suit well enough with the French; for as
20 we, who are a more sullen people, come to be
diverted at our plays, so they, who are of an airy
and gay temper, come thither to make themselves
more serious: and this I conceive to be one reason
why comedies are [4] more pleasing to us, and tragedies
25 to them.   But to speak generally: it cannot be denied
that short speeches and replies are more apt to move
the passions and beget concernment in us, than the

---

*Formerly an hour-glass was fixed on the pulpit in all our
churches. (Malone.)

[1] the tedious, A.   [2] as our Parsons do, A.
[3] an hundred or two hundred lines, A.
[4] so C; Comedy's are, B; Comedy is, A.

other; for it is unnatural for any one in a gust of
passion to speak long together, or for another in the
same condition to suffer him, without interruption.
Grief and passion are like floods raised in little
brooks by a sudden rain; they are quickly up; and 5
if the concernment be poured unexpectedly in upon
us, it overflows us: but a long sober shower gives
them leisure to run out as they came in, without
troubling the ordinary current. As for comedy, repartee is one of its chiefest graces; the greatest 10
pleasure of the audience is a chace of wit, kept up
on both sides, and swiftly managed. And this our
forefathers, if not we, have had in Fletcher's plays,
to a much higher degree of perfection than the
French poets can reasonably hope to reach[1].   15

'There is another part of Lisideius his discourse,
in which he has rather excused our neighbours, than
commended them; that is, for aiming only to make
one person considerable in their plays. 'Tis very
true what he has urged, that one character in all 20
plays, even without the poet's care, will have advantage of all the others; and that the design of the
whole drama will chiefly depend on it. But this
hinders not that there may be more shining characters
in the play: many persons of a second magnitude, 25
nay, some so very near, so almost equal to the first,
that greatness may be opposed to greatness, and all
the persons be made considerable, not only by their
quality, but their action. 'Tis evident that the more
the persons are, the greater will be the variety of the 30
plot. If then the parts are managed so regularly,

[1] can arrive at, A.

that the beauty of the whole be kept entire, and that the variety become not a perplexed and confused mass of accidents, you will find it infinitely pleasing to be led in a labyrinth of design, where you see
5 some of your way before you, yet discern not the end till you arrive at it. And that all this is practicable, I can produce for examples many of our English plays : as *The Maid's Tragedy, The Alchemist, The Silent Woman* : I was going to have named *The*
10 *Fox*[n], but that the unity of design seems not exactly observed in it; for there appear[1] two actions in the play; the first naturally ending with the fourth act; the second forced from it in the fifth : which yet is the less to be condemned in him, because the dis-
15 guise of Volpone, though it suited not with his character as a crafty or covetous person, agreed well enough with that of a voluptuary; and by it the poet gained the end at which he aym'd[2], the punishment of vice, and the reward of virtue, both[3] which that
20 disguise produced. So that to judge equally of it, it was an excellent fifth act, but not so naturally proceeding from the former.

But to leave this, and pass to the latter part of Lisideius his discourse, which concerns relations :
25 I must acknowledge with him, that the French have reason to hide[4] that part of the action which would occasion too much tumult on the stage, and to choose[5] rather to have it made known by narration to the audience. Farther, I think it very convenient, for
30 the reasons he has given, that all incredible actions

---

[1] appears, A.   [2] the end he aym'd at, A.   [3] A *om.* both.
[4] when they hide, A.   [5] and choose, A.

were removed; but, whether custom has so insinu-
ated itself into our countrymen, or nature has so
formed them to fierceness, I know not; but they will
scarcely suffer combats and other objects of horrour
to be taken from them. And indeed, the indecency 5
of tumults is all which can be objected against
fighting: for why may not our imagination as well
suffer itself to be deluded with the probability of it,
as with any other thing in the play? For my part,
I can with as great ease persuade myself that the 10
blows[1] are given in good earnest, as I can, that they
who strike them are kings or princes, or those persons
which they represent. For objects of incredibility,—
I would be satisfied from Lisideius, whether we have
any so removed from all appearance of truth, as are 15
those of Corneille's *Andromede*[n]; a play which has
been frequented the most of any he has writ. If
the Perseus, or the son of an heathen god, the
Pegasus, and the Monster, were not capable to choke
a strong belief, let him blame any representation of 20
ours hereafter. Those indeed were objects of delight; yet the reason is the same as to the probability:
for he makes it not a Ballette[2] or masque, but a play,
which is to resemble truth. But for death, that it
ought not to be represented, I have, besides the 25
arguments alledged by Lisideius, the authority of
Ben Johnson, who has forborn it in his tragedies;
for both the death of Sejanus and Catiline are related: though in the latter I cannot but observe one
irregularity of that great poet; he has removed the 30
scene in the same act from Rome to Catiline's army,

---

[1] the blowes which are struck, A.   [2] Balette, C.

and from thence again to Rome; and besides, has
allowed a very inconsiderable time, after Catiline's
speech, for the striking of the battle, and the return
of Petreius, who is to relate the event of it to the
5 senate : which I should not animadvert on him, who
was otherwise a painful observer of τὸ πρέπον, or the
decorum of the stage, if he had not used extreme
severity in his judgment on the incomparable
Shakspeare for the same fault [n].—To conclude on
10 this subject of relations ; if we are to be blamed for
shewing too much of the action, the French are as
faulty for discovering too little of it : a mean betwixt
both should be observed by every judicious writer,
so as the audience may neither be left unsatisfied by
15 not seeing what is beautiful, or shocked by beholding
what is either incredible or undecent.

'I hope I have already proved in this discourse,
that though we are not altogether so punctual as the
French, in observing the laws of comedy, yet our
20 errours are so few, and little, and those things
wherèin we excel them so considerable, that we
ought of right to be preferred before them. But
what will Lisideius say, if they themselves acknowledge they are too strictly bounded[1] by those laws,
25 for breaking which he has blamed the English?
I will alledge Corneille's words, as I find them in
the end of his Discourse of the three Unities :—*Il
est facile aux speculatifs d'estre severes &c.* "'Tis
easy for speculative persons to judge severely; but
30 if they would produce to publick view ten or twelve
pieces of this nature, they would perhaps give more

---

[1] ti'd up, A.

latitude to the rules than I have done, when, by experience, they had known how much we are limited[1]
and constrained by them, and how many beauties
of the stage they banished from it." To illustrate a
little what he has said :—By their servile observations 5
of the unities of time and place, and integrity of
scenes, they have brought on themselves that dearth
of plot, and narrowness of imagination, which may
be observed in all their plays. How many beautiful
accidents might naturally happen in two or three 10
days, which cannot arrive with any probability in
the compass of twenty-four hours? There is time
to be allowed also for maturity of design, which,
amongst great and prudent persons, such as are
often represented in tragedy, cannot, with any likeli- 15
hood of truth, be brought to pass at so short a warning. Farther; by tying themselves strictly to the
unity of place, and unbroken scenes, they are forced
many times to omit some beauties which cannot be
shewn where the act began ; but might, if the scene 20
were interrupted, and the stage cleared for the persons
to enter in another place ; and therefore the French
poets are often forced upon absurdities ; for if the
act begins in a chamber, all the persons in the play
must have some business or other to come thither, 25
or else they are not to be shewn that act ; and sometimes their characters are very unfitting to appear
there : as, suppose it were the king's bed-chamber ;
yet the meanest man in the tragedy must come and
dispatch his business there, rather than in the lobby 30
or courtyard, (which is fitter for him,) for fear the

---

[1] bound up, A.

stage should be cleared, and the scenes broken. Many times they fall by it in a greater inconvenience; for they keep their scenes unbroken, and yet change the place; as in one of their newest plays, where the
5 act begins in the street. There a gentleman is to meet his friend; he sees him with his man, coming out from his father's house; they talk together, and the first goes out: the second, who is a lover, has made an appointment with his mistress; she appears
10 at the window, and then we are to imagine the scene lies under it. This gentleman is called away, and leaves his servant with his mistress; presently her father is heard from within; the young lady is afraid the servingman should be discovered, and thrusts him
15 into a place of safety[1], which is supposed to be her closet. After this, the father enters to the daughter, and now the scene is in a house; for he is seeking from one room to another for this poor Philipin, or French Diego[n], who is heard from within, drolling
20 and breaking many a miserable conceit on the subject of his sad[2] condition. In this ridiculous manner the play goes forward[3], the stage being never empty all the while: so that the street, the window, the houses, and the closet, are made to walk about, and the per-
25 sons to stand still. Now what, I beseech you, is more easy than to write a regular French play, or more difficult than to write an irregular English one, like those of Fletcher, or of Shakspeare?

'If they content themselves, as Corneille did, with
30 some flat design, which, like an ill riddle, is found

---

[1] for 'into a place of safety,' A has 'in through a door.'
[2] upon his sad, A.   [3] goes on, A.

out ere it be half proposed, such plots we can make
every way regular, as easily as they; but whenever
they endeavour to rise to any quick turns and coun-
terturns of plot, as some of them have attempted,
since Corneille's plays have been less in vogue, you 5
see they write as irregularly as we, though they cover
it more speciously.   Hence the reason is perspicuous,
why no French plays, when translated, have, or ever
can succeed on the English stage.   For, if you consider the plots, our own are fuller of variety; if the 10
writing, ours are more quick and fuller of spirit; and
therefore 'tis a strange mistake in those who decry
the way of writing plays in verse, as if the English
therein imitated the French.   We have borrowed
nothing from them; our plots are weaved in English 15
looms: we endeavour therein to follow the variety
and greatness of characters which are derived to us
from Shakspeare and Fletcher; the copiousness and
well-knitting of the intrigues we have from Johnson;
and for the verse itself we have English precedents 20
of elder date than any of Corneille's plays.   Not to
name our old comedies before Shakspeare, which
were all writ in verse of six feet, or Alexandrines[n],
such as the French now use,—I can shew in Shakspeare, many scenes of rhyme together, and the like 25
in Ben Johnson's tragedies: in *Catiline* and *Sejanus*
sometimes thirty or forty lines,—I mean besides the
Chorus, or the monologues; which, by the way,
shewed Ben no enemy to this way of writing, especially if you read[1] his *Sad Shepherd*[n], which goes 30
sometimes on rhyme, sometimes on blank verse, like

---

[1] look upon, A.

F

an horse who eases himself on trot and amble.   You
find him likewise commending Fletcher's pastoral of
*The Faithful Shepherdess*ⁿ, which is for the most part
rhyme, though not refined to that purity to which it hath
5 since been brought.   And these examples are enough
to clear us from a servile imitation of the French.

   'But to return whence[1] I have digressed: I dare
boldly affirm these two things of the English drama;
—First, that we have many plays of ours as regular
10 as any of theirs, and which, besides, have more
variety of plot and characters; and secondly, that in
most of the irregular plays of Shakspeare or Fletcher,
(for Ben Johnson's are for the most part regular,)
there is a more masculine fancy and greater spirit in
15 the writing, than there is in any of the French.   I
could produce, even in Shakspeare's and Fletcher's
works, some plays which are almost exactly formed;
as *The Merry Wives of Windsor*ⁿ, and *The Scornful
Lady*: but because (generally speaking) Shakspeare,
20 who writ first, did not perfectly observe the laws of
comedy, and Fletcher, who came nearer to perfection,
yet through carelessness made many faults; I will
take the pattern of a perfect play from Ben Johnson,
who was a careful and learned observer of the dra-
25 matick laws, and from all his comedies I shall select
The Silent Woman; of which I will make a short
examen, according to those rules which the French
observe.'

   As Neander was beginning to examine *The Silent
30 Woman*, Eugenius, earnestly regarding him[2]; 'I
beseech you, Neander,' said he, 'gratify the company,

---

[1] from whence, A.   [2] looking earnestly upon him, A.

and me in particular, so far, as before you speak of
the play, to give us a character of the author; and
tell us frankly your opinion, whether you do not
think all writers, both French and English, ought to
give place to him.'   5

'I fear,' replied Neander, 'that in obeying your
commands I shall draw some envy[1] on myself.
Besides, in performing them, it will be first necessary
to speak somewhat of Shakspeare and Fletcher, his
rivals in poesy; and one of them, in my opinion, 10
at least his equal, perhaps[n] his superior.

'To begin, then, with Shakspeare. He was the
man who of all modern, and perhaps ancient poets,
had the largest and most comprehensive soul. All
the images of nature were still present to him, and 15
he drew them, not laboriously, but luckily; when
he describes any thing, you more than see it, you
feel it too. Those who accuse him to have wanted
learning, give him the greater commendation: he
was naturally learned; he needed not the spectacles 20
of books to read nature; he looked inwards, and
found her there. I cannot say he is every where
alike; were he so, I should do him injury to compare
him with the greatest of mankind. He is many
times flat, insipid; his comick wit degenerating into 25
clenches, his serious swelling into bombast. But
he is always great, when some great occasion is
presented to him; no man can say he ever had a fit
subject for his wit, and did not then raise himself
as high above the rest of poets,   30

Quantum lenta solent inter viburna cupressi.[n]

[1] a little envy, A.

F 2

The consideration of this made Mr. Hales of Eaton
say, that there was no subject of which any poet ever
writ, but he would produce it much better done[1] in
Shakspeare; and however others are now generally
5 preferred before him, yet the age wherein he lived,
which had contemporaries with him Fletcher and
Johnson, never equalled them to him in their esteem :
and in the last king's court, when Ben's reputation
was at highest, Sir John Suckling, and with him the
10 greater part of the courtiers, set our Shakspeare far
above him.

'Beaumont and Fletcher, of whom I am next to
speak, had, with the advantage of Shakspeare's wit,
which was their precedent, great natural gifts, im-
15 proved by study : Beaumont especially being so accurate a judge of plays, that Ben Johnson, while he
lived, submitted all his writings to his censure, and,
'tis thought, used his judgment in correcting, if not
contriving, all his plots.   What value he had for him,
20 appears by the verses he writ to him ; and therefore
I need speak no farther of it.   The first play that
brought Fletcher and him in esteem was their *Philaster*[n] : for before that, they had written two or three
very unsuccessfully, as the like is reported of Ben
25 Johnson, before he writ *Every Man in his Humour.*
Their plots were generally more regular than Shakspeare's, especially those which were made before
Beaumont's death* ; and they understood and imitated

[1] treated of, A.

* Sir Aston Cokain long since complained, that the booksellers
who, in 1647, published thirty-four plays under the names of
Beaumont and Fletcher, had not ascertained how many of them
were written solely by Fletcher :

the conversation of gentlemen much better; whose
wild debaucheries, and quickness of wit in reparties,
no poet before them could paint[1] as they have done.
Humour, which[2] Ben Johnson derived from particular
persons, they made it not their business to describe: 5
they represented all the passions very lively, but above
all, love. I am apt to believe the English language
in them arrived to its highest perfection : what words
have since been taken in, are rather superfluous than
ornamental[3]. Their plays[n] are now the most pleasant 10
and frequent entertainments of the stage; two of
theirs being acted through the year for one of Shakspeare's or Johnson's: the reason is, because there is
a certain gaiety in their comedies, and pathos in their
more serious plays, which suits generally with all 15
men's humours. Shakspeare's language is likewise
a little obsolete, and Ben Johnson's wit comes short
of theirs.

As for Johnson, to whose character I am now
arrived, if we look upon him while he was himself, 20
(for his last plays were but his dotages,) I think him
the most learned and judicious writer which any
theatre ever had. He was a most severe judge of
himself, as well as others. One cannot say he wanted
wit, but rather that he was frugal of it. In his works 25

> 'In the large book of plays you late did print,
> In Beaumont's and in Fletcher's name, why in't
> Did you not justice? give to each his due?
> For Beaumont of those many writ in few;
> And Massinger in other few: the main
> Being sole issues of sweet Fletcher's brain.' (Malone.)

[1] for ' before them could paint ' A has ' can ever paint.'
[2] This Humour of which, A.   [3] necessary, A.

you find little to retrench or alter. Wit, and language, and humour also in some measure, we had before him; but something of art was wanting to the drama, till he came. He managed his strength to more
5 advantage than any who preceded him. You seldom find him making love in any of his scenes, or endeavouring to move the passions; his genius was too sullen and saturnine to do it gracefully, especially when he knew he came after those who had per-
10 formed both to such an height. Humour was his proper sphere; and in that he delighted most to represent mechanick people. He was deeply conversant in the ancients, both Greek and Latin, and he borrowed boldly from them: there is scarce a poet
15 or historian among the Roman authors of those times whom he has not translated in *Sejanus* and *Catiline*. But he has done his robberies so openly, that one may see he fears not to be taxed by any law. He invades authors like a monarch; and what would be
20 theft in other poets, is only victory in him. With the spoils of these writers he so represents old Rome to us, in its rites, ceremonies, and customs, that if one of their poets had written either of his tragedies, we had seen less of it than in him. If there was any fault in
25 his language, 'twas that he weaved it too closely and laboriously, in his comedies especially[1]: perhaps too, he did a little too much Romanize our tongue, leaving the words which he translated almost as much Latin as he found them: wherein, though he learnedly fol-
30 lowed their[2] language, he did not enough comply with

---

[1] for 'comedies especially' A has 'serious Playes.'
[2] the idiom of their, A.

the idiom of ours. If I would compare him with Shakspeare, I must acknowledge him the more correct poet, but Shakspeare the greater wit. Shakspeare was the Homer, or father of our dramatick poets; Johnson was the Virgil, the pattern of elaborate 5 writing; I admire him, but I love Shakspeare. To conclude of him; as he has given us the most correct plays, so in the precepts which he has laid down in his *Discoveries*[n], we have as many and profitable rules for perfecting the stage, as any wherewith the French 10 can furnish us.

'Having thus spoken of the author, I proceed to the examination of his comedy, *The Silent Woman*[n].

EXAMEN OF THE SILENT WOMAN.

'To begin first with the length of the action; it 15 is so far from exceeding the compass of a natural day, that it takes not up an artificial one. 'Tis all included in the limits of three hours and an half, which is no more than is required for the presentment on the stage: a beauty perhaps not much observed; 20 if it had, we should not have looked on the Spanish translation of *Five Hours* * with so much wonder. The scene of it is laid in London; the latitude of place is almost as little as you can imagine; for it lies all within the compass of two houses, and after 25 the first act, in one. The continuity of scenes is observed more than in any of our plays, except his own *Fox* and *Alchemist.* They are not broken above twice or thrice at most in the whole comedy; and in the two best of Corneille's plays, the *Cid* and *Cinna*, 30

* See p. 55.

they are interrupted once[1]. The action of the play is entirely one ; the end or aim of which is the settling Morose's estate on Dauphine. The intrigue of it is the greatest and most noble of any pure unmixed
5 comedy in any language ; you see in it many persons of various characters and humours, and all delightful. As first, Morose, or an old man, to whom all noise but his own talking is offensive. Some who would be thought criticks, say this humour of his is forced :
10 but to remove that objection, we may consider him first to be naturally of a delicate hearing, as many are, to whom all sharp sounds are unpleasant ; and secondly, we may attribute much of· it to the peevishness of his age, or the wayward authority of an old
15 man in his own house, where he may make himself obeyed ; and to this the poet seems to allude[2] in his name Morose. Besides this, I am assured from divers persons, that Ben Johnson was actually acquainted with such a man, one altogether as ridiculous as he is
20 here represented. Others say, it is not enough to find one man of such an humour ; it must be common to more, and the more common the more natural. To prove this, they instance in the best of comical characters, Falstaff. There are many men resembling
25 him ; old, fat, merry, cowardly, drunken, amorous, vain, and lying. But to convince these people, I need but tell them, that humour is the ridiculous extravagance of conversation, wherein one man differs from all others. If then it be common, or communi-
30 cated to many, how differs it from other men's ? or what indeed causes it to be ridiculous so much as the

[1] once apiece, A.   [2] this . . . seems to allude to, A.

singularity of it? As for Falstaff, he is not properly
one humour, but a miscellany of humours or images,
drawn from so many several men : that wherein he is
singular is his wit[1], or those things he says *præter
expectatum,* unexpected by the audience ; his quick 5
evasions, when you imagine him surprised, which,
as they are extremely diverting of themselves, so
receive a great addition from his person ; for the
very sight of such an unwieldy old debauched fellow
is a comedy alone. And here, having a place so 10
proper for it, I cannot but enlarge somewhat upon this
subject of humour into which I am fallen. The
ancients had little of it in their comedies ; for the
τὸ γελοῖον[n] of the old comedy, of which Aristophanes
was chief, was not so much to imitate a man, as to 15
make the people laugh at some odd conceit, which
had commonly somewhat of unnatural or obscene in
it. Thus, when you see Socrates brought upon the
stage, you are not to imagine him made ridiculous
by the imitation of his actions, but rather by making 20
him perform something very unlike himself; something so childish and absurd, as by comparing it with
the gravity of the true Socrates, makes a ridiculous
object for the spectators. In their new comedy which
succeeded, the poets sought indeed to express the 25
ἦθος, as in their tragedies the πάθος of mankind[n]. But
this ἦθος contained only the general characters of men
and manners ; as old men, lovers, serving-men, cour-
tezans, parasites, and such other persons as we see
in their comedies ; all which they made alike : that is, 30
one old man or father, one lover, one courtezan, so

[1] in his wit, A.

like another, as if the first of them had begot the rest
of every sort: *Ex homine hunc natum dicas.* The
same custom they observed likewise in their tragedies.
As for the French, though they have the word *humeur*
5 among them, yet they have small use of it in their
comedies or farces ; they being but ill imitations of
the *ridiculum,* or that which stirred up laughter in the
old comedy. But among the English 'tis otherwise :
where by humour is meant some extravagant habit,
10 passion, or affection, particular (as I said before) to
some one person, by the oddness of which, he is
immediately distinguished from the rest of men ;
which being lively and naturally represented, most
frequently begets that malicious pleasure in the
15 audience which is testified by laughter; as all things
which are deviations from customs[1] are ever the aptest
to produce it : though by the way this laughter is only
accidental, as the person represented is fantastick or
bizarre ; but pleasure is essential to it, as the imitation
20 of what is natural. The description of these humours,
drawn from the knowledge and observation of particular persons, was the peculiar genius and talent of
Ben Johnson; to whose play I now return.

' Besides Morose, there are at least nine or ten dif-
25 ferent characters and humours in *The Silent Woman* ;
all which persons have several concernments of their
own, yet are all used by the poet, to the conducting
of the main design to perfection. I shall not waste
time in commending the writing of this play; but I
30 will give you my opinion, that there is more wit and
acuteness of fancy in it than in any of Ben Johnson's.

---

[1] common customes, A.

Besides that he has here described the conversation
of gentlemen in the persons of True-Wit, and his
friends, with more gaiety, air, and freedom, than in
the rest of his comedies. For the contrivance of the
plot, 'tis extreme¹ elaborate, and yet withal easy; for 5
the λύσις², or untying of it, 'tis so admirable, that when
it is done, no one of the audience would think the
poet could have missed it; and yet it was concealed
so much before the last scene, that any other way
would sooner have entered into your thoughts. But 10
I dare not take upon me to commend the fabrick of it,
because it is altogether so full of art, that I must un-
ravel every scene in it to commend it as I ought.
And this excellent contrivance is still the more to be
admired, because 'tis comedy, where the persons are 15
only of common rank, and their business private, not
elevated by passions or high concernments, as in
serious plays. Here every one is a proper judge of
all he sees, nothing is represented but that with which
he daily converses: so that by consequence all faults 20
lie open to discovery, and few are pardonable. 'Tis
this which Horace has judiciously observed:

> *Creditur, ex medio quia res arcessit, habere*
> *Sudoris minimum; sed habet Comedia tanto*
> *Plus oneris, quanto veniæ minus.* ⁿ   25

But our poet who was not ignorant of these difficulties,
has made use³ of all advantages; as he who designs
a large leap takes his rise from the highest ground.
One of these advantages is that which Corneille has
laid down as the greatest which can arrive to any 30

---

¹ so C; extream, A and B.   ² δέσις, A.
³ had prevailed himself, A.

poem, and which he himself could never compass above thrice in all his plays ; viz. the making choice of some signal and long-expected day, whereon the action of the play is to depend.   This day was that
5 designed by Dauphine for the settling of his uncle's estate upon him ; which to compass, he contrives to marry him.   That the marriage had been plotted by him long beforehand, is made evident by what he tells True-wit in the second act, that in one moment
10 he had destroyed what he had been raising many months.

'There is another artifice of the poet, which I cannot here omit, because by the frequent practice of it in his comedies he has left it to us almost as a
15 rule ; that is, when he has any character or humour wherein he would shew a *coup de Maistre,* or his highest skill, he recommends it to your observation by a pleasant description of it before the person first appears.   Thus, in *Bartholomew-Fair*[n] he gives you
20 the pictures of Numps and Cokes, and in this those of Daw, Lafoole, Morose, and the Collegiate Ladies ; all which you hear described before you see them. So that before they come upon the stage, you have a longing expectation of them, which prepares you
25 to receive them favourably ; and when they are there, even from their first appearance you are so far ac-quainted with them, that nothing of their humour is lost to you.

'I will observe yet one thing further of this admir-
30 able plot ; the business of it rises in every act.   The second is greater than the first ; the third than the second ; and so forward to the fifth.   There too you

see, till the very last scene, new difficulties arising to
obstruct the action of the play; and when the audience
is brought into despair that the business can naturally
be effected, then, and not before, the discovery is
made.   But that the poet might entertain you with 5
more variety all this while, he reserves some new
characters to shew you, which he opens not till the
second and third act; in the second Morose, Daw,
the Barber, and Otter; in the third the Collegiate
Ladies : all which he moves afterwards in by-walks, 10
or under-plots, as diversions to the main design, lest
it should grow tedious, though they are still naturally
joined with it, and somewhere or other subservient to
it.   Thus, like a skilful chess-player[1], by little and
little he draws out his men, and makes his pawns 15
of use to his greater persons.

'If this comedy[n] and some others of his, were
translated into French prose, (which would now be
no wonder to them, since Moliere has lately given
them plays out of verse, which have not displeased 20
them,) I believe the controversy would soon be decided betwixt the two nations, even making them
the judges.   But we need not call our heroes[2] to
our aid.   Be it spoken to the honour of the English,
our nation can never want in any age such who are 25
able to dispute the empire of wit with any people
in the universe.   And though the fury of a civil
war, and power for twenty years together aban-
doned to a barbarous race of men, enemies of all
good learning, had buried the muses under the 30

---

[1] so C; Chest-player, A and B.
[2] so C; Hero's, A and B.

ruins of monarchy; yet, with the restoration of our happiness, we see revived poesy lifting up its head, and already shaking off the rubbish which lay so heavy on it. We have seen since his majesty's 5 return, many dramatick poems which yield not to those of any foreign nation, and which deserve all laurels but the English. I will set aside flattery and envy: it cannot be denied but we have had some little blemish either in the plot or writing of all those 10 plays which have been made within these seven years; (and perhaps there is no nation in the world so quick to discern them, or so difficult to pardon them, as ours:) yet if we can persuade ourselves to use the candour of that poet, who, though the most severe 15 of criticks, has left us this caution by which to moderate our censures—

>——*ubi plura nitent in carmine, non ego paucis
>Offendar maculis ;—*[n]

if, in consideration of their many and great beauties, 20 we can wink at some slight and little imperfections, if we, I say, can be thus equal to ourselves, I ask no favour from the French. And if I do not venture upon any particular judgment of our late plays, 'tis out of the consideration which an ancient writer gives 25 me: *vivorum, ut magna admiratio, ita censura difficilis*[n]: betwixt the extremes of admiration and malice, 'tis hard to judge uprightly of the living. Only I think it may be permitted me to say, that as it is no lessening to us to yield to some plays, and those not many, 30 of our own nation in the last age, so can it be no addition to pronounce of our present poets, that they have far surpassed all the ancients, and the modern writers of other countries [1].'

This was [2] the substance of what was then spoke on that occasion ; and Lisideius, I think, was going to reply, when he was prevented thus by Crites: 'I am confident,' said he, 'that the most material things that can be said have been already urged on either side ; if they have not, I must beg of Lisideius that he will defer his answer till another time: for I confess I have a joint quarrel to you both, because you have concluded, without any reason given for it, that rhyme is proper for the stage. I will not dispute how ancient it hath been among us to write this way ; perhaps our ancestors knew no better till Shakspeare's time. I will grant it was not altogether left by him, and that Fletcher and Ben Johnson used it frequently in their Pastorals, and sometimes in other plays. Farther,—I will not argue whether we received it originally from our own countrymen, or from the French ; for that is an inquiry of as little benefit, as theirs who, in the midst of the late plague [3], were not so solicitous to provide against it, as to know whether we had it from the malignity of our own air, or by transportation from Holland. I have therefore only to affirm, that it is not allowable in serious plays ; for comedies, I find you already concluding with me. To prove this, I might satisfy myself to tell you, how much in vain it is for you to strive against the stream of the people's inclination ; the greatest part of which are prepossessed so much

---

[1] so C; Countreys, A and B.   [2] This, my Lord, was, A.
[3] the great plague, A.

with those excellent plays of Shakspeare, Fletcher,
and Ben Johnson, which have been written out of
rhyme, that except you could bring them such as
were written better in it, and those too by persons
5 of equal reputation with them, it will be impossible
for you to gain your cause with them, who will still
be judges.   This it is to which, in fine, all your
reasons must submit.   The unanimous consent of an
audience is so powerful, that even Julius Cæsar, (as
10 Macrobius reports of him,) when he was perpetual
dictator, was not able to balance it on the other side;
but when Laberius, a Roman Knight, at his request
contended in the *Mime* with another poet [n], he was
forced to cry out, *Etiam favente me victus es, Laberi*[1].
15 But I will not on this occasion take the advantage of
the greater number, but only urge such reasons against
rhyme, as I find in the writings of those who have ar-
gued for the other way.   First then, I am of opinion,
that rhyme is unnatural in a play, because dialogue
20 there is presented as the effect of sudden thought:
for a play is the imitation of nature; and since no
man, without premeditation speaks in rhyme, neither
ought he to do it on the stage.   This hinders not but
the fancy may be there elevated to an higher pitch of
25 thought than it is in ordinary discourse; for there is
a probability that men of excellent and quick parts
may speak noble things *extempore*: but those thoughts
are never fettered with the numbers or sound of verse
without study, and therefore it cannot be but unnatural
30 to present the most free way of speaking in that which
is the most constrained.   For this reason, says Aris-

---

[1] Liberi, A.

totle[n], 'tis best to write tragedy in that kind of verse which is the least such, or which is nearest prose: and this amongst the ancients was the Iambick, and with us is blank verse, or the measure of verse kept exactly without rhyme. These numbers therefore are 5 fittest for a play; the others for a paper of verses, or a poem; blank verse being as much below them, as rhyme is improper for the drama. And if it be objected that neither are blank verses made *extempore*, yet, as nearest nature, they are still to be preferred. 10 —But there are two particular exceptions, which many besides myself have had to verse; by which it will appear yet more plainly how improper it is in plays. And the first of them is grounded on that very reason for which some have commended rhyme; they say, 15 the quickness of repartees in argumentative scenes receives an ornament from verse. Now what is more unreasonable than to imagine that a man should not only light upon the wit[1], but the rhyme too, upon the sudden? This nicking of him who spoke before both 20 in sound and measure, is so great an happiness, that you must at least suppose the persons of your play to be born poets: *Arcades omnes, et cantare pares, et respondere parati*[n]: they must have arrived to the degree of *quicquid conabar dicere*;—to make verses almost 25 whether they will or no. If they are any thing below this, it will look rather like the design of two, than the answer of one: it will appear that your actors hold intelligence together; that they perform their tricks like fortune-tellers, by confederacy. The hand 30 of art will be too visible in it, against that maxim

---

[1] so A; not only imagine the Wit, B.

of all professions—*Ars est celare artem*; that it is the
greatest perfection of art to keep itself undiscovered.
Nor will it serve you to object, that however you
manage it, 'tis still known to be a play; and, conse-
5 quently, the dialogue of two persons understood to
be the labour of one poet.   For a play is still an
imitation of nature; we know we are to be deceived,
and we desire to be so; but no man ever was deceived
but with a probability of truth; for who will suffer a
10 gross lie to be fastened on him?   Thus we sufficiently
understand, that the scenes which represent cities and
countries to us are not really such, but only painted
on boards and canvas; but shall that excuse the ill
painture or designment of them?   Nay, rather ought
15 they not to be laboured with so much the more diligence and exactness, to help the imagination? since
the mind of man does naturally tend to[1] truth; and
therefore the nearer any thing comes to the imitation
of it, the more it pleases.

20   'Thus, you see, your rhyme is uncapable of expressing the greatest thoughts naturally, and the
lowest it cannot with any grace: for what is more
unbefitting the majesty of verse, than to call a
servant, or bid a door be shut in rhyme? and yet
25 you are often forced on this miserable necessity[2].   But
verse, you say, circumscribes a quick and luxuriant
fancy, which would extend itself too far on every
subject, did not the labour which is required to well-
turned and polished rhyme, set bounds to it.   Yet
30 this argument, if granted, would only prove that we

---

[1] tend to and seek after, A.
[2] this mis. nec. you are forc'd upon, A.

may write better in verse, but not more naturally. Neither is it able to evince that; for he who wants judgment to confine his fancy in blank verse, may want it as much in rhyme: and he who has it will avoid errors in both kinds. Latin verse was as great 5 a confinement to the imagination of those poets, as rhyme to ours; and yet you find Ovid saying too much on every subject. *Nescivit* (says Seneca) *quod bene cessit relinquere* [n] : of which he gives you one famous instance in his description of the deluge : 10

> *Omnia pontus erat, deerant quoque litora ponto* [n].
> Now all was sea, nor had that sea a shore.

Thus Ovid's fancy was not limited by verse, and Virgil needed not verse to have bounded his.

'In our own language we see Ben Johnson con- 15 fining himself to what ought to be said, even in the liberty of blank verse; and yet Corneille, the most judicious of the French poets, is still varying the same sense an hundred ways, and dwelling eternally on the same subject, though confined by rhyme. 20 Some other exceptions I have to verse; but since these[1] I have named are for the most part already publick, I conceive it reasonable they should first be answered.'

'It concerns me less than any,' said Neander, 25 (seeing he had ended,) 'to reply to this discourse; because when I should have proved that verse may be natural in plays, yet I should always be ready to confess, that those which I have written in this kind [n] come short of that perfection which is required. Yet 30

---

[1] but being these, A.

(Howard)

since you are pleased I should undertake this province, I will do it, though with all imaginable respect
and deference, both to that person [n] from whom you
have borrowed your strongest arguments, and to
5 whose judgment, when I have said all, I finally
submit. But before I proceed to answer your objections, I must first remember you, that I exclude
all comedy from my defence; and next that I deny
not but blank verse may be also used; and content
10 myself only to assert, that in serious plays where the
subject and characters are great, and the plot unmixed with mirth, which might allay or divert these
concernments which are produced, rhyme is there as
natural and more effectual than blank verse.
15   'And now having laid down this as a foundation,
—to begin with Crites,—I must crave leave to tell
him, that some of his arguments against rhyme reach
no farther than, from the faults or defects of ill rhyme,
to conclude against the use of it in general. May not
20 I conclude against blank verse by the same reason?
If the words of some poets who write in it, are either
ill chosen, or ill placed, which makes not only rhyme,
but all kind of verse in any language unnatural, shall
I, for their vicious affectation, condemn those excellent
25 lines of Fletcher, which are written in that kind? Is
there any thing in rhyme more constrained than this
line in blank verse?—*I heaven invoke, and strong
resistance make*; where you see both the clauses are
placed unnaturally, that is, contrary to the common
30 way of speaking, and that without the excuse of a
rhyme to cause it: yet you would think me very
ridiculous, if I should accuse the stubbornness of

blank verse for this, and not rather the stiffness of
the poet. Therefore, Crites, you must either prove
that words, though well chosen, and duly placed, yet
render not rhyme natural in itself; or that, however
natural and easy the rhyme may be, yet it is not 5
proper for a play. If you insist on the former part, I
would ask you, what other conditions are required to
make rhyme natural in itself, besides an election of
apt words, and a right disposition[1] of them? For
the due choice of your words expresses your sense 10
naturally, and the due placing them adapts the rhyme
to it. If you object that one verse may be made for
the sake of another, though both the words and rhyme
be apt, I answer, it cannot possibly so fall out; for
either there is a dependance of sense betwixt the first 15
line and the second, or there is none: if there be
that connection, then in the natural position of the
words the latter line must of necessity flow from the
former; if there be no dependance, yet still the due
ordering of words makes the last line as natural in 20
itself as the other: so that the necessity of a rhyme
never forces any but bad or lazy writers to say what
they would not otherwise. 'Tis true, there is both
care and art required to write in verse. A good poet
never establishes[2] the first line, till he has sought out 25
such a rhyme as may fit the sense, already prepared
to heighten the second: many times the close of the
sense falls into the middle of the next verse, or farther
off, and he may often prevail himself[n] of the same
advantages in English which Virgil had in Latin,—he 30
may break off in the hemystich, and begin another

---

[1] disposing, A.   [2] concludes upon, A.

line. Indeed, the not observing these two last things, makes plays which are writ in verse, so tedious : for though, most commonly, the sense is to be confined to the couplet, yet nothing that does *perpetuo tenore* 5 *fluere*, run in the same channel, can please always. 'Tis like the murmuring of a stream, which not varying in the fall, causes at first attention, at last drowsiness. Variety of cadences is the best rule ; the greatest help to the actors, and refreshment to 10 the audience.

'If then verse may be made natural in itself, how becomes it unnatural in[1] a play? You say the stage is the representation of nature, and no man in ordinary conversation speaks in rhyme. But you foresaw 15 when you said this, that it might be answered—neither does any man speak in blank verse, or in measure without rhyme. Therefore you concluded, that which is nearest nature is still to be preferred. But you took no notice that rhyme might be made as natural 20 as blank verse, by the well placing of the words, &c. All the difference between them, when they are both correct, is, the sound in one, which the other wants ; and if so, the sweetness of it, and all the advantage resulting from it, which are handled in the Preface to 25 *The Rival Ladies*, will yet stand good. As for that place of Aristotle, where he says, plays should be writ in that kind of verse which is nearest prose, it makes little for you ; blank verse being properly but measured prose. Now measure alone, in any modern 30 language, does not constitute verse ; those of the ancients in Greek and Latin consisted in quantity of

---

[1] improper to, A.

words, and a determinate number of feet. But when,
by the inundation of the Goths and Vandals into
Italy, new languages were introduced[1], and barba-
rously mingled with the Latin, of which the Italian,
Spanish, French, and ours, (made out of them and 5
the Teutonick,) are dialects, a new way of poesy was
practised; new, I say, in those countries, for in all
probability it was that of the conquerors in their own
nations: at least we are able to prove, that the eastern
people have used it from all antiquity[2]. This new 10
way consisted in measure or number of feet, and
rhyme; the sweetness of rhyme, and observation of
accent, supplying the place of quantity in words,
which could neither exactly be observed by those
barbarians, who knew not the rules of it, neither was 15
it suitable to their tongues, as it had been to the
Greek and Latin. No man is tied in modern poesy
to observe any farther rule in the feet of his verse,
but that they be dissyllables; whether Spondee,
Trochee, or Iambick, it matters not; only he is 20
obliged to rhyme: neither do the Spanish, French,
Italian, or Germans, acknowledge at all, or very rarely,
any such kind of poesy as blank verse amongst them.
Therefore, at most 'tis but a poetick prose, a *sermo
pedestris*; and as such, most fit for comedies, where 25
I acknowledge rhyme to be improper.—Farther; as
to that quotation of Aristotle, our couplet verses may
be rendered as near prose as blank verse itself, by
using those advantages I lately named,—as breaks in
an hemistich, or running the sense into another line,— 30

[1] brought in, A.
[2] A *om.* at least ... antiquity, and the note.

thereby making art and order appear as loose and free as nature : or not tying ourselves to couplets strictly, we may use the benefit of the Pindarick way practised in *The Siege of Rhodes*[n]; where the numbers vary, and
5 the rhyme is disposed carelessly, and far from often chyming. Neither is that other advantage of the ancients to be despised, of changing the kind of verse when they please, with the change of the scene, or some new entrance ; for they confine not themselves
10 always to iambicks, but extend their liberty to all lyrick numbers, and sometimes even to hexameter. But I need not go so far to prove that rhyme, as it succeeds to all other offices of Greek and Latin verse, so especially to this of plays, since the custom of
15 nations[1] at this day confirms it ; the French[2], Italian, and Spanish tragedies are generally writ in it ; and sure the universal consent of the most civilized parts of the world, ought in this, as it doth in other customs, to[3] include the rest.
20 　'But perhaps you may tell me, I have proposed such a way to make rhyme natural, and consequently proper to plays, as is unpracticable ; and that I shall scarce find six or eight lines together in any play, where the words are so placed and chosen as is re-
25 quired to make it natural. I answer, no poet need constrain himself at all times to it. It is enough he makes it his general rule ; for I deny not but some-times there may be a greatness in placing the words otherwise ; and sometimes they may sound better ;
30 sometimes also the variety itself is excuse enough. But if, for the most part, the words be placed as they

---

[1] all Nations, A.　　　[2] all the French, &c., A.　　　[3] A *om.* to.

are in the negligence of prose, it is sufficient to de-
nominate the way practicable ; for we esteem that to
be such, which in the trial oftner succeeds than misses.
And thus far you may find the practice made good
in many plays : where you do not, remember still, that 5
if you cannot find six natural rhymes together, it
will be as hard for you to produce as many lines in
blank verse, even among the greatest of our poets,
against which I cannot make some reasonable ex-
ception.   10

'And this, Sir, calls to my remembrance the beginning of your discourse, where you told us we
should never find the audience favourable to this
kind of writing, till we could produce as good plays
in rhyme, as Ben Johnson, Fletcher, and Shakspeare, 15
had writ out of it.   But it is to raise envy to the
living, to compare them with the dead.   They are
honoured, and almost adored by us, as they deserve ;
neither do I know any so presumptuous of themselves
as to contend with them.   Yet give me leave to say 20
thus much, without injury to their ashes ; that not
only we shall never equal them, but they could never
equal themselves, were they to rise and write again.
We acknowledge them our fathers in wit ; but they
have ruined their estates themselves, before they came 25
to their children's hands.   There is scarce an humour,
a character, or any kind of plot, which they have not
used[1].   All comes sullied or wasted to us : and were
they to entertain this age, they could not now[2] make
so plenteous treatments out of such decayed fortunes. 30
This therefore will be a good argument to us, either

---

[1] blown upon, A.   [2] A *om.*

not to write at all, or to attempt some other way. There is no bays to be expected in their walks: *tentanda via est, quà me quoque possum tollere humo* [n].

This way of writing in verse they have only left free to us; our age is arrived to a perfection in it, which they never knew; and which (if we may guess by what of theirs we have seen in verse, as *The Faithful Shepherdess*, and *Sad Shepherd*) 'tis probable they never could have reached. For the genius of every age is different; and though ours excel in this, I deny not but to imitate nature in that perfection which they did in prose, is a greater commendation than to write in verse exactly. As for what you have added—that the people are not generally inclined to like this way, —if it were true, it would be no wonder, that betwixt the shaking off an old habit, and the introducing of a new, there should be difficulty. Do we not see them stick to Hopkins' and Sternhold's psalms, and forsake those of David, I mean Sandys his translation [n] of them? If by the people you understand the multitude, the οἱ πολλοί, 'tis no matter what they think; they are sometimes in the right, sometimes in the wrong: their judgment is a mere lottery. *Est ubi plebs rectè putat, est ubi peccat* [n]. Horace says it of the vulgar, judging poesy. But if you mean the mixed audience of the populace and the noblesse, I dare confidently affirm that a great part of the latter sort are already favourable to verse; and that no serious plays written since the king's return have been more kindly received by them, than *The Siege of Rhodes*, the *Mustapha* [n], *The Indian Queen*, and *Indian Emperor*.

'But I come now to the inference of your first

argument. You said that[1] the dialogue of plays is
presented as the effect of sudden thought, but no man
speaks suddenly, or *extempore*, in rhyme ; and you inferred from thence, that rhyme, which you acknowledge
to be proper to epick poesy, cannot equally be proper 5
to dramatick, unless we could suppose all men born
so much more than poets, that verses should be made
in them, not by them.

' It has been formerly urged by you, and confessed
by me, that since no man spoke any kind of verse 10
extempore, that which was nearest nature was to be
preferred. I answer you, therefore, by distinguishing
betwixt what is nearest to the nature of comedy, which
is the imitation of common persons and ordinary
speaking, and what is nearest the nature of a serious 15
play : this last is indeed the representation of nature,
but 'tis nature wrought up to an higher pitch. The
plot, the characters, the wit, the passions, the descriptions, are all exalted above the level of common
converse, as high as the imagination of the poet can 20
carry them, with proportion to verisimility. Tragedy,
we know, is wont to image to us the minds and fortunes of noble persons, and to portray these exactly ;
heroick rhyme is nearest nature, as being the noblest
kind of modern verse. 25

> *Indignatur enim privatis et prope socco*
> *Dignis carminibus narrari cœna Thyestæ*[n]—

says Horace : and in another place,

> *Effutire leves indigna tragœdia versus*[n]—.

Blank verse is acknowledged to be too low for a 30

---

[1] A *om.*

poem, nay more, for a paper of verses ; but if too low
for an ordinary sonnet, how much more for tragedy,
which is by Aristotle, in the dispute betwixt the epick
poesy and the dramatick, for many reasons he there
5 alledges, ranked above it ?

'But setting this defence aside, your argument is
almost as strong against the use of rhyme in poems
as in plays ; for the epick way is every where interlaced with dialogue, or discoursive scenes ; and
10 therefore you must either grant rhyme to be improper there, which is contrary to your assertion, or
admit it into plays by the same title which you have
given it to poems. For though tragedy be justly
preferred above the other, yet there is a great affinity
15 between them, as may easily be discovered in that
definition of a play which Lisideius gave us. The
genus of them is the same,—a just and lively image
of human nature, in its actions, passions, and tra-
verses of fortune : so is the end,—namely, for the
20 delight and benefit of mankind. The characters and
persons are still the same, viz. the greatest of both
sorts ; only the manner of acquainting us with those
actions, passions, and fortunes, is different. Tragedy
performs it *viva voce*, or by action, in dialogue ;
25 wherein it excels the epick poem, which does it
chiefly by narration, and therefore is not so lively
an image of human nature. However, the agree-
ment betwixt them is such, that if rhyme be proper
for one, it must be for the other. Verse, 'tis true,
30 is not the effect of sudden thought ; but this hinders
not that sudden thought may be represented in verse,
since those thoughts are such as must be higher

than nature can raise them without premeditation, especially to a continuance of them, even out of verse; and consequently you cannot imagine them to have been sudden either in the poet or in the actors. A play, as I have said, to be like nature, is to be set 5 above it; as statues which are placed on high are made greater than the life, that they may descend to the sight in their just proportion.

'Perhaps I have insisted too long on this objection; but the clearing of it will make my stay shorter on 10 the rest. You tell us, Crites, that rhyme appears most unnatural in repartees, or short replies: when he who answers, (it being presumed he knew not what the other would say, yet) makes up that part of the verse which was left incomplete, and supplies 15 both the sound and measure of it. This, you say, looks rather like the confederacy of two, than the answer of one.

'This, I confess, is an objection which is in every man's[1] mouth, who loves not rhyme: but suppose, 20 I beseech you, the repartee were made only in blank verse, might not part of the same argument be turned against you? for the measure is as often supplied there, as it is in rhyme; the latter half of the hemistich as commonly made up, or a second line sub- 25 joined as a reply to the former; which any one leaf in Johnson's plays will sufficiently clear to you. You will often find in the Greek tragedians, and in Seneca, that when a scene grows up into the warmth of repartees, which is the close fighting of it, the 30 latter part of the trimeter is supplied by him who

---

[1] ones, A.

answers; and yet it was never observed as a fault
in them by any of the ancient or modern cricks.
The case is the same in our verse, as it was in
theirs; rhyme to us being in lieu of quantity to
them.   But if no latitude is to be allowed a poet,
you take from him not only his licence of *quidlibet
audendi,* but you tie him up in a straiter compass
than you would a philosopher.   This is indeed
Musas colere severiores. You would have him follow
nature, but he must follow her on foot : you have dis-
mounted him from his Pegasus.   But you tell us, this
supplying the last half of a verse, or adjoining a whole
second to the former, looks more like the design of
two, than the answer of one.   Suppose we acknowledge it : how comes this confederacy to be more
displeasing to you, than in a dance which is well
contrived ?   You see there the united design of
many persons to make up one figure : after they
have separated themselves in many petty divisions,
they rejoin one by one into a gross : the confederacy
is plain amongst them, for chance could never produce any thing so beautiful ; and yet there is nothing
in it, that shocks your sight.   I acknowledge the hand
of art appears in repartee, as of necessity it must in
all kind of verse.   But there is also the quick and
poynant brevity of it (which is an high imitation of
nature in those sudden gusts of passion) to mingle
with it ; and this, joined with the cadency and sweetness of the rhyme, leaves nothing in the soul of the
hearer to desire.   'Tis an art which appears ; but it
appears only like the shadowings of painture, which
being to cause the rounding of it, cannot be absent ;

but while that is considered, they are lost : so while
we attend to the other beauties of the matter, the care
and labour of the rhyme is carried from us, or at least
drowned in its own sweetness, as bees are sometimes
buried in their honey. When a poet has found the 5
repartee, the last perfection he can add to it, is to put
it into verse. However good the thought may be,
however apt the words in which 'tis couched, yet he
finds himself at a little unrest, while rhyme is wanting : he cannot leave it till that comes naturally, and 10
then is at ease, and sits down contented [n].

' From replies, which are the most elevated thoughts
of verse, you pass to those which are most mean, and
which [1] are common with the lowest of houshold conversation. In these, you say, the majesty of verse 15
suffers. You instance in the calling of a servant, or
commanding a door to be shut, in rhyme. This,
Crites, is a good observation of your's, but no argument : for it proves no more but that such thoughts
should be waved, as often as may be, by the address 20
of the poet. But suppose they are necessary in the
places where he uses them, yet there is no need to
put them into rhyme. He may place them in the
beginning of a verse, and break it off, as unfit, when
so debased, for any other use ; or granting the worst, 25
—that they require more room than the hemistich
will allow, yet still there is a choice to be made of
the best words, and least vulgar, (provided they be
apt,) to express such thoughts. Many have blamed
rhyme in general, for this fault, when the poet with 30
a little care might have redressed it. But they do it

---

[1] to the most mean ones, those which, A.

with no more justice, than if English poesy should
be made ridiculous for the sake of the Water-poet's [n]
rhymes. Our language is noble, full, and significant ;
and I know not why he who is master of it may not
5 clothe ordinary things in it as decently as the Latin,
if he use the same diligence in his choice of words :
delectus verborum origo est eloquentiæ [n]. It was the
saying of Julius Cæsar, one so curious in his, that
none of them can be changed but for a worse.   One
10 would think, *unlock the door*, was a thing as vulgar as
could be spoken; and yet Seneca could make it sound
high and lofty in his Latin :

Reserate clusos regii postes laris [n].
Set wide the palace gates.

15   'But I turn from this exception, both because it
happens not above twice or thrice in any play that
those vulgar thoughts are used ; and then too, (were
there no other apology to be made, yet,) the necessity
of them, which is alike in all kind of writing, may
20 excuse them.   For if they are little and mean in
rhyme, they are of consequence such in blank verse [1].
Besides that the great eagerness and precipitation
with which they are spoken, makes us rather mind
the substance than the dress ; that for which they are
25 spoken, rather than what is spoke.   For they are
always the effect of some hasty concernment, and
something of consequence depends on them.

    'Thus, Crites, I have endeavoured to answer your
objections ; it remains only that I should vindicate
30 an argument for verse, which you have gone about to

---

[1] A *om.* For if they . . . blank verse.

overthrow. It had formerly been said, that the easiness of blank verse renders the poet too luxuriant, but that the labour of rhyme bounds and circumscribes an over-fruitful fancy; the sense[1] there being commonly confined to the couplet, and the words so 5 ordered that the rhyme naturally follows them, not they the rhyme. To this you answered, that it was no argument to the question in hand; for the dispute was not which way a man may write best, but which is most proper for the subject on which he writes. 10

'First, give me leave, Sir, to remember you, that the argument against which you raised this objection, was only secondary: it was built on this hypothesis, —that to write in verse was proper for serious plays. Which supposition being granted, (as it was briefly 15 made out in that discourse, by shewing how verse might be made natural,) it asserted, that this way of writing was an help to the poet's judgment, by putting bounds to a wild overflowing fancy. I think, therefore, it will not be hard for me to make good 20 what it was to prove on that supposition[2]. But you add, that were this let pass, yet he who wants judgment in the liberty of his fancy, may as well shew the defect of it when he is confined to verse; for he who has judgment will avoid errors, and he who has 25 it not, will commit them in all kinds of writing.

This argument, as you have taken it from a most acute person, so I confess it carries much weight in it: but by using the word judgment here indefinitely, you seem to have put a fallacy upon us. I grant, he 30 who has judgment, that is, so profound, so strong,

---

[1] so A; scene, B and C.   [2] A *om.* on that supposition.

H

or rather [1] so infallible a judgment, that he needs no
helps to keep it always poised and upright, will commit no faults either in rhyme or out of it. And on
the other extreme, he who has a judgment so weak
5 and crazed that no helps can correct or amend it,
shall write scurvily out of rhyme, and worse in it.
But the first of these judgments is no where to be
found, and the latter is not fit to write at all. To
speak therefore of judgment as it is in the best poets;
10 they who have the greatest proportion of it, want
other helps than from it, within. As for example,
you would be loth to say, that he who is [2] endued
with a sound judgment has [3] no need of history,
geography, or moral philosophy, to write correctly.
15 Judgment is indeed the master-workman in a play;
but he requires many subordinate hands, many tools
to his assistance. And verse I affirm to be one of
these; 'tis a rule and line by which he keeps his
building compact and even, which otherwise lawless
20 imagination would raise either irregularly or loosely;
at least, if the poet commits errors with this help, he
would make greater and more without it :—'tis, in
short, a slow and painful, but the surest kind of
working. Ovid, whom you accuse for luxuriancy
25 in verse, had perhaps been farther guilty of it, had
he writ in prose. And for your instance of Ben
Johnson, who, you say, writ exactly without the
help of rhyme; you are to remember, 'tis only an
aid to a luxuriant fancy, which his was not: as he
30 did not want imagination, so none ever said he
had much to spare. Neither was verse then re-

---

[1] A *om.* or rather.   [2] was, A.   [3] had, A.

fined so much, to be an help to that age, as it is to
ours. Thus then the second thoughts being usually
the best, as receiving the maturest digestion from
judgment, and the last and most mature product of
those thoughts being artful and laboured verse, it 5
may well be inferred, that verse is a great help to
a luxuriant fancy; and this is what that argument
which you opposed was to evince.'

Neander was pursuing this discourse so eagerly,
that Eugenius had called to him twice or thrice, ere 10
he took notice that the barge stood still, and that they
were at the foot of Somerset-stairs, where they had
appointed it to land. The company were all sorry to
separate so soon, though a great part of the evening
was already spent; and stood a-while looking back on 15
the water, upon which the moon-beams played[1], and
made it appear like floating quicksilver: at last they
went up through a crowd of French people, who were
merrily dancing in the open air, and nothing concerned for the noise of guns which had alarmed the 20
town that afternoon. Walking thence together to the
Piazze[n], they parted there; Eugenius and Lisideius
to some pleasant appointment they had made, and
Crites and Neander to their several lodgings.

[1] which the moon beams played upon, A.

A DEFENCE[1]

OF DRAMATIC POESY*.

THE former edition of *The Indian Emperor* being full of faults, which had escaped the printer, I have been willing to overlook this second with more care; and though I could not allow myself so much time as was necessary, yet, by that little I have done, the press is freed from some gross errors which it had to answer

[1] The text of the 'Defence' is reprinted from the original edition of 1668 (the only one published in Dryden's life-time), a copy of which is in the British Museum; it is prefixed as a sort of Introduction to the *second* edition of Dryden's *Indian Emperor*.

* Our author married, probably about the year 1664, Lady Elizabeth Howard, sister of Sir Robert Howard knt., and daughter of Thomas, the first Earl of Berkshire [ancestor of the present Earl of Suffolk]. In 1660 he had addressed some complimentary verses to Sir Robert, which were prefixed to his poems, published in 8vo. in that year. In 1666 they appear to have been on good terms; Dryden having then addressed to him an encomiastick Epistle in prose, which is dated from Charleton, in Wiltshire (the seat of the Earl of Berkshire), and was prefixed to his *Annus Mirabilis*, published in 8vo. in 1667, by Sir Robert Howard, who revised the sheets at the press for the author, who was then in the country; and in the Epistle he describes him as one whom he knew not to be of the number of those, *qui carpere amicos suos judicium vocant.* In the *Essay on Dramatick Poesy*, as we have already seen, he speaks of Sir Robert Howard with great respect. That gentleman, how-

for before. As for the more material faults of writing, which are properly mine, though I see many of them, I want leisure to amend them. 'Tis enough for those who make one poem the business of their lives, to leave that correct: yet, excepting Virgil, I never met 5 with any which was so in any language.

But while I was thus employed about this impression, there came to my hands a new printed play, called, *The Great Favourite, or The Duke of Lerma*; the author of which, a noble and most ingenious 10 person, has done me the favour to make some observations and animadversions upon my *Dramatique Essay*. I must confess he might have better consulted his reputation, than by matching himself with so weak an adversary. But if his honour be diminished in the 15 choice of his antagonist, it is sufficiently recompensed in the election of his cause: which being the weaker, in all appearance, as combating the received opinions of the best ancient and modern authors, will add to his glory, if he overcome, and to the opinion of his 20

ever, having in 1668 published [in the preface to his tragedy, *The Duke of Lerma*] reflections on the Essay, our author retorted in the following observations, which are found prefixed to the second edition of *The Indian Emperor*, published in the same year. In many copies, however, of that edition, they are wanting; nor were they reprinted in any other edition of that play which appeared in the life-time of the author: so that it should seem he was induced by good nature, or the interposition of friends, to suppress this witty and severe replication. One of the lampoons of the time gives a more invidious turn to this suppression, and insinuates that he was compelled to retract. They lived afterwards probably in good correspondence together; at least, it appears from an original letter of our author now before me, that towards the close of his life they were on friendly terms. (Malone.)

generosity, if he be vanquished : since he ingages at so great odds, and, so like a cavalier, undertakes the protection of the weaker party.   I have only to fear on my own behalf, that so good a cause as mine may 5 not suffer by my ill management, or weak defence ; yet I cannot in honour but take the glove, when 'tis offered me : though I am only a champion by suc-cession ; and no more able to defend the right of Aristotle and Horace, than an infant Dimock to main-10 tain the title of a King.

For my own concernment in the controversie, it is so small, that I can easily be contented to be driven from a few notions of Dramatique Poesie ; especially by one, who has the reputation of understanding all 15 things : and I might justly make that excuse for my yielding to him, which the Philosopher made to the Emperor,—*why should I offer to contend with him, who is master of more than twenty legions of arts and sciences ?*   But I am forced to fight, and therefore it 20 will be no shame to be overcome.

Yet I am so much his servant, as not to meddle with any thing which does not concern me in his Preface ; therefore, I leave the good sense and other excellencies of the first twenty lines to be considered 25 by the critiques.   As for the play of *The Duke of Lerma*, having so much altered and beautified it, as he has done, it can justly belong to none but him. Indeed, they must be extream ignorant as well as envious, who would rob him of that honour ; for you see 30 him putting in his claim to it, even in the first two lines :

Repulse upon repulse, like waves thrown back,
That slide to hang upon obdurate rocks.

After this, let detraction do its worst; for if this be not his, it deserves to be. For my part, I declare for distributive justice; and from this and what follows, he certainly deserves *those advantages which he acknowledges to have received from the opinion of sober* men.

In the next place, I must beg leave to observe his great address in courting the reader to his party. For intending to assault all poets, both ancient and modern, he discovers not his whole design at once, but seems only to aim at me, and attacques me on my weakest side, my defence of verse.

To begin with me,—he gives me the compellation of *The Author of a Dramatique Essay*, which is a little discourse in dialogue, for the most part borrowed from the observations of others: therefore, that I may not be wanting to him in civility, I return his compliment by calling him *The Author of The Duke of Lerma.*

But (that I may pass over his salute) he takes notice of my great pains to prove rhyme as natural in a serious play, and more effectual than blanck verse. Thus, indeed, I did state the question; but he tells me, *I pursue that which I call natural in a wrong application: for 'tis not the question whether rhyme or not rhyme be best or most natural for a serious subject, but what is nearest the nature of that it represents.*

If I have formerly mistaken the question, I must confess my ignorance so far, as to say I continue still in my mistake: but he ought to have proved that I mistook it; for it is yet but *gratis dictum:* I still shall

think I have gained my point, if I can prove that
rhyme is best or most natural for a serious subject.
As for the question as he states it, whether rhyme be
nearest the nature of what it represents, I wonder he
5 should think me so ridiculous as to dispute whether
prose or verse be nearest to ordinary conversation.

It still remains for him to prove his inference,—
that, since verse is granted to be more remote than
prose from ordinary conversation, therefore no serious
10 plays ought to be writ in verse: and when he clearly
makes that good, I will acknowledge his victory as
absolute as he can desire it.

The question now is, which of us two has mistaken
it; and if it appear I have not, the world will suspect
15 *what gentleman that was, who was allowed to speak
twice in parliament, because he had not yet spoken to
the question*; and perhaps conclude it to be the same,
who, 'tis reported, maintained a contradiction *in ter-
minis*, in the face of three hundred persons.

20   But to return to verse; whether it be natural or not
in plays, is a problem which is not demonstrable of
either side: 'tis enough for me that he acknowledges
he had rather read good verse than prose: for if all
the enemies of verse will confess as much, I shall not
25 need to prove that it is natural, I am satisfied, if it
cause delight: for delight is the chief, if not the only,
end of poesie: instruction can be admitted but in the
second place; for poesie only instructs as it delights.

'Tis true, that to imitate well is a poet's work; but to
30 affect the soul, and excite the passions, and above all
to move admiration, which is the delight of serious
plays, a bare imitation will not serve.   The converse,

therefore, which a poet is to imitate, must be heightened
with all the arts and ornaments of poesie ; and must
be such, as, strictly considered, could never be supposed spoken by any without premeditation.

As for what he urges, that *a play will still be sup-* 5
posed to be a composition of several persons speaking ex
tempore ; *and that good verses are the hardest things*
which can be imagined to be so spoken ; I must crave
leave to dissent from his opinion, as to the former
part of it : for, if I am not deceived, a play is supposed 10
to be the work of the poet, imitating or representing
the conversation of several persons ; and this I think
to be as clear, as he thinks the contrary.

But I will be bolder, and do not doubt to make it
good, though a paradox, that one great reason why 15
prose is not to be used in serious plays, is, because it
is too near the nature of converse : there may be too
great a likeness ; as the most skilful painters affirm,
that there may be too near a resemblance in a picture :
to take every lineament and feature, is not to make an 20
excellent piece ; but to take so much only as will
make a beautiful resemblance of the whole ; and, with
an ingenious flattery of nature, to heighten the beauties
of some parts, and hide the deformities of the rest.
For so says Horace :   25

> *Ut pictura poesis erit......*
> *Hæc amat obscurum, vult hæc sub luce videri,*
> *Judicis argutum quæ non formidat acumen*[n].
> ————————————— *et quæ*
> *Desperat tractata nitescere posse, relinquit*[n].   30

In *Bartholomew Fair,* or the lowest kind of comedy,
that degree of heightning is used, which is proper to

set off that subject. 'Tis true the author was not there to go out of prose, as he does in his higher arguments of comedy, *The Fox*, and *Alchymist*; yet he does so raise his matter in that prose, as to render
5 it delightful ; which he could never have performed, had he only said or done those very things that are daily spoken or practised in the Fair; for then the Fair itself would be as full of pleasure to an ingenious person as the play; which we manifestly see it is not.
10 But he hath made an excellent lazar[n] of it : the copy is of price, though the original be vile.   You see in *Catiline* and *Sejanus*, where the argument is great, he sometimes ascends to verse, which shews he thought it not unnatural in serious plays : and had his genius
15 been as proper for rhyme, as it was for humour, or had the age in which he lived attained to as much knowledge in verse as ours, it is probable he would have adorned those subjects with that kind of writing.
20   Thus prose, though the rightful prince, yet is by common consent deposed, as too weak for the government of serious plays ; and he failing, there now start up two competitors ; one the nearer in blood, which is blanck verse; the other more fit for the ends
25 of government, which is rhyme.   Blanck verse is, indeed, the nearer prose, but he is blemished with the weakness of his predecessor.   Rhyme (for I will deal clearly) has somewhat of the usurper in him ; but he is brave and generous, and his dominion
30 pleasing.   For this reason of delight, the Ancients (whom I will still believe as wise as those who so confidently correct them) wrote all their tragedies in

verse, though they knew it most remote from conversation.

But I perceive I am falling into the danger of
another rebuke from my opponent; for when I plead
that the Ancients used verse, I prove not that they 5
would have admitted rhyme, had it then been written:
all I can say is only this; that it seems to have succeeded verse by the general consent of poets in all
modern languages: for almost all their serious plays
are written in it: which, though it be no demonstra- 10
tion that therefore they ought to be so, yet at least
the practice first, and then the continuation of it,
shews that it attained the end,—which was to please;
and if that cannot be compassed here, I will be the
first who shall lay it down.   For I confess my chief 15
endeavours are to delight the age in which I live.   If
the humour of this be for low comedy, small accidents, and raillery, I will force my genius to obey it,
though with more reputation I could write in verse.
I know I am not so fitted by nature to write comedy: 20
I want that gayety of humour which is required to it.
My conversation is slow and dull, my humour saturnine and reserved: in short, I am none of those who
endeavour to break jests in company, or make reparties.   So that those who decry my comedies do me no 25
injury, except it be in point of profit: reputation in
them is the last thing to which I shall pretend.   I
beg pardon for entertaining the reader with so ill
a subject; but before I quit that argument, which was
the cause of this digression, I cannot but take notice 30
how I am corrected for my quotation of Seneca, in my
defence of plays in verse.   My words are these: 'Our

language is noble, full, and significant; and I know
not why he who is master of it, may not cloath ordinary things in it as decently as the Latine, if he use
the same diligence in his *choice of words.*   One would
5 think, *unlock a door,* was a thing as vulgar as could be
spoken; yet Seneca could make it sound high and
lofty in his Latin:

Reserate clusos regii postes laris.'

But he says of me, *That being filled with the prece-*
10 *dents of the Ancients, who writ their plays in verse,*
I commend the thing; declaring our language to be full,
noble, and significant, and charging all defects upon the
ill placing of words, *which I prove by quoting Seneca*
loftily expressing such an ordinary thing as shutting a
15 door.

Here he manifestly mistakes; for I spoke not
of the placing, but of the choice of words; for
which I quoted that aphorism of Julius Cæsar:

Delectus verborum est origo eloquentiæ:

20 but *delectus verborum* is no more Latin for the placing
of words, than *reserate* is Latin for *shut the door,*
as he interprets it, which I ignorantly construed
unlock or *open* it.

He supposes I was highly affected with the sound
25 of those words; and I suppose I may more justly
imagine it of him; for if he had not been extreamly
satisfied with the sound, he would have minded the
sense a little better.

But these are now to be no faults; for ten days
30 after his book is published, and that his mistakes are
grown so famous that they are come back to him, he

sends his *Errata** to be printed, and annexed to his
play; and desires, that instead of *shutting* you would
read *opening*; which, it seems, was the printer's fault.
I wonder at his modesty, that he did not rather say it
was Seneca's, or mine ; and that in some authors, 5
reserare was to *shut* as well as to *open*, as the word
barach, say the learned, is both to *bless* and *curse.*

Well, since it was the printer, he was a naughty
man to commit the same mistake twice in six lines : I
warrant you *delectus verborum* for *placing of words* 10
was his mistake too, though the author forgot to tell
him of it : if it were my book, I assure you I should.
For those rascals ought to be the proxies of every
gentleman author, and to be chastised for him, when
he is not pleased to own an errour. Yet since he 15
has given the *Errata*, I wish he would have inlarged
them only a few sheets more, and then he would have
spared me the labour of an answer : for this cursed
printer is so given to mistakes, that there is scarce
a sentence in the Preface without some false grammar 20
or hard sense in it ; which will all be charged upon
the poet, because he is so good-natured as to lay but
three errours to the printer's account, and to take the
rest upon himself, who is better able to support them.
But he needs not apprehend that I should strictly 25
examine those little faults, except I am called upon to
do it : I shall return therefore to that quotation of
Seneca, and answer, not to what he writes, but to
what he means. I never intended it as an argument,
but only as an illustration of what I had said before 30

* This *erratum* has been suffered to remain in the edition of the
knight's plays now before us, published in 1692. (Scott.)

concerning the election of words: and all he can charge me with is only this,—that if Seneca could make an ordinary thing sound well in Latin by the choice of words, the same, with the like care, might
5 be performed in English: if it cannot, I have committed an errour on the right hand, by commending too much the copiousness and well-sounding of our language; which I hope my countrymen will pardon me. At least the words which follow in my Dramatique
10 Essay will plead somewhat in my behalf; for I say there, that this objection happens but seldom in a play; and then too either the meanness of the expression may be avoided, or shut out from the verse by breaking it in the midst.

15 But I have said too much in the defence of verse; for after all, it is a very indifferent thing to me, whether it obtain or not. I am content hereafter to be ordered by his rule, that is, to write it sometimes, because it pleases me; and so much the rather,
20 because he has declared that it pleases him. But he has taken his last farewell of the Muses, and he has done it civilly, by honouring them with the name of *his long acquaintances*; which is a complement[1] they have scarce deserved from him. For my own
25 part, I bear a share in the publick loss; and how emulous soever I may be of his fame and reputation, I cannot but give this testimony of his style,—that it is extream poetical, even in oratory; his thoughts elevated sometimes above common apprehension; his
30 notions politick and grave, and tending to the instruction of princes, and reformation of states; that

[1] sic.

they are abundantly interlaced with variety of fancies, tropes, and figures, which the criticks have enviously branded with the name of obscurity and false grammar.

Well, he is now fettered in business of more unpleasant nature: the Muses have lost him, but the commonwealth gains by it; the corruption of a poet is the generation of a statesman.

He will not venture again into the civil wars of censure; ubi . . . nullos habitura triumphos [n]: if he had not told us he had left the Muses, we might have half suspected it by that word, *ubi*, which does not any way belong to them in that place; the rest of the verse is indeed Lucan's; but that *ubi*, I will answer for it, is his own. Yet he has another reason for this disgust of Poesie; for he says immediately after, that *the manner of plays which are now in most esteem, is beyond his power to perform*: to perform the manner of a thing, I confess is new English to me. *However, he condemns not the satisfaction of others; but rather their unnecessary understanding, who, like Sancho Pança's doctor, prescribe too strictly to our appetites; for*, says he, *in the difference of* Tragedy *and* Comedy, *and of* Farce *itself, there can be no determination but by the taste, nor in the manner of their composure.*

We shall see him now as great a critick as he was a poet; and the reason why he excelled so much in poetry will be evident, for it will appear to have proceeded from the exactness of his judgment. *In the difference of Tragedy, Comedy, and Farce itself, there can be no determination but by the taste.* I will not quarrel with the obscurity of his phrase, though I justly might; but beg his pardon if I do not rightly understand him: if he means, that there is no essential difference betwixt comedy, tragedy, and farce, but what is only made by the 5 people's taste, which distinguishes one of them from the other, that is so manifest an errour, that I need not lose time to contradict it. Were there neither judge, taste, nor opinion in the world, yet they would differ in their natures; for the action, character, 10 and language of tragedy, would still be great and high; that of comedy lower and more familiar; admiration would be the delight of one, and satyr of the other.

I have but briefly touched upon these things, 15 because, whatever his words are, I can scarce imagine, that *he who is always concerned for the true honour of reason, and would have no spurious issue fathered upon her*, should mean any thing so absurd as to affirm, *that there is no difference betwixt comedy and* 20 *tragedy, but what is made by the taste only*: unless he would have us understand the comedies of my Lord L*, where the first act should be pottages, the second Fricassees, &c. and the fifth a *chere entiere* of women.

25 I rather guess he means, that betwixt one comedy or tragedy and another, there is no other difference but what is made by the liking or disliking of the audience. This is indeed a less errour than the former, but yet it is a great one. The liking or 30 disliking of the people gives the play the denomina-

---

* I suppose lord Lauderdale. He was not created a duke till 1672. (Malone.)

tion of good or bad; but does not really make or
constitute it such. To please the people ought to
be the poet's aim, because plays are made for their
delight; but it does not follow that they are always
pleased with good plays, or that the plays which 5
please them are always good. The humour of the
people is now for comedy; therefore, in hope to
please them, I write comedies rather than serious
plays; and so far their taste prescribes to me : but
it does not follow from that reason, that comedy is 10
to be preferred before tragedy in its own nature; for
that which is so in its own nature cannot be otherwise; as a man cannot but be a rational creature:
but the opinion of the people may alter, and in
another age, or perhaps in this, serious plays may 15
be set up above comedies.

This I think a sufficient answer : if it be not, he
has provided me of an excuse; it seems, in his
wisdom, he foresaw my weakness, and has found
out this expedient for me, *That it is not necessary for* 20
poets to study strict reason ; since they are so used to
a greater latitude than is allowed by that severe in-
quisition, that they must infringe their own jurisdiction,
to profess themselves obliged to argue well.

I am obliged to him for discovering to me this 25
back-door; but I am not yet resolved on my retreat :
for I am of opinion that they cannot be good poets,
who are not accustomed to argue well. False
reasonings and colours of speech are the certain
marks of one who does not understand the stage ; 30
for moral truth is the mistress of the poet, as much
as of the philosopher. Poesie must resemble natural

I

truth, but it must *be* ethical.   Indeed the poet dresses
truth, and adorns nature, but does not alter them :

Ficta voluptatis causâ sint proxima veris[n].

Therefore, that is not the best poesy, which re-
5 sembles notions of things that are not to things that
are : though the fancy may be great, and the words
flowing, yet the soul is but half satisfied when there
is not truth in the foundation.   This is that which
makes Virgil be preferred before the rest of Poets :
10 in variety of fancy and sweetness of expression,
you see Ovid far above him ; for Virgil rejected
many of those things which Ovid wrote.   *A great
wit's great work is to refuse*, as my worthy friend,
Sir John Berkenhead, has ingeniously expressed it :
15 you rarely meet with any thing in Virgil but truth,
which therefore leaves the strongest impression of
pleasure in the soul.   This I thought myself obliged
to say in behalf of Poesie ; and to declare, though it
be against myself, that when poets do not argue well,
20 the defect is in the workman, not in the art.

And now I come to the boldest part of his discourse, wherein he attacques not me, but all the
ancients and moderns ; and undermines, as he thinks,
the very foundations on which Dramatique Poesie is
25 built.   I could wish he would have declined that envy
which must of necessity follow such an undertaking,
and contented himself with triumphing over me in my
opinions of verse, which I will never hereafter dispute
with him ; but he must pardon me, if I have that
30 veneration for Aristotle, Horace, Ben Johnson, and
Corneille, that I dare not serve him in such a cause,

and against such heroes, but rather fight under their
protection, as Homer reports of little Teucer, who
shot the Trojans from under the large buckler of
Ajax Telamon :

Στῆ δ' ἄρ' ὑπ' Αἴαντος σάκεϊ Τελαμωνιάδαο[n]. 5

He stood beneath his brother's ample shield,
And cover'd there, shot death through all the field,

The words of my noble adversary are these :

*But if we examine the general rules laid down for
plays by strict reason, we shall find the errours equally* 10
*gross ; for the great foundation which is laid to build
upon, is nothing, as it is generally stated, as will appear
upon the examination of the particulars.*

These particulars, in due time, shall be examined :
in the mean while, let us consider what this great 15
foundation is, which he says is nothing, as it is
generally stated. I never heard of any other foundation of Dramatique Poesie than the imitation of
nature ; neither was there ever pretended any other
by the ancients, or moderns, or me, who endeavour 20
to follow them in that rule. This I have plainly
said in my definition of a play ; that it is a just and
lively image of human nature, &c. Thus the foundation, as it is generally stated, will stand sure, if
this definition of a play be true ; if it be not, he 25
ought to have made his exception against it, by
proving that a play is not an imitation of nature,
but somewhat else which he is pleased to think it.

But it is very plain, that he has mistaken the
foundation for that which is built upon it, though 30

I 2

not immediately : for the direct and immediate consequence is this ; if nature be to be imitated, then
there is a rule for imitating nature rightly ; otherwise
there may be an end, and no means conducing to it.
5 Hitherto I have proceeded by demonstration ; but
as our divines, when they have proved a Deity,
because there is order, and have inferred that this
Deity ought to be worshipped, differ afterwards
in the manner of the worship ; so, having laid
10 down that nature is to be imitated, and that proposition proving the next, that then there are means
which conduce to the imitating of nature, I dare
proceed no farther positively ; but have only laid
down some opinions of the ancients and moderns,
15 and of my own, as means which they used, and
which I thought probable for the attaining of that
end.   Those means are the same which my antagonist calls the foundations,—how properly, the world
may judge ; and to prove that this is his meaning,
20 he clears it immediately to you, by enumerating those
rules or propositions against which he makes his
particular exceptions,—as namely, those of time, and
place,—in these words : *First, we are told the plot*
should not be so ridiculously contrived, as to crowd two
25 *several countries into one stage ; secondly, to cramp the*
accidents of many years or days into the representation
of two hours and an half; and lastly, a conclusion
drawn, that the only remaining dispute is, concerning
time, whether it should be contained in twelve or twenty-
30 *four hours ; and the place to be limited to that spot*
of ground where the play is supposed to begin : and
this is called nearest nature ; for that is concluded most

natural, which is most probable, and nearest to that which it presents.

Thus he has only made a small mistake of the means conducing to the end, for the end itself; and of the superstructure for the foundation : but he pro- 5 ceeds : *To shew, therefore, upon what ill grounds they dictate laws for Dramatique Poesie,* &c. He is here pleased to charge me with being magisterial, as he has done in many other places of his Preface. There- fore in vindication of myself, I must crave leave to 10 say, that my whole discourse was sceptical, according to that way of reasoning which was used by Socrates, Plato, and all the Academicques of old, which Tully and the best of the ancients followed, and which is imitated by the modest inquisitions of the Royal 15 Society. That it is so, not only the name will shew, which is, *An Essay,* but the frame and composition of the work. You see, it is a dialogue sustained by persons of several opinions, all of them left doubtful, to be determined by the readers in general ; and 20 more particularly defer'd to the accurate judgment of my lord Buckhurst, to whom I made a dedication of my book. These are my words in my Epistle, speaking of the persons whom I introduced in my dialogue : It is true, they differed in their opinions, 25 as it is probable they would ; neither do I take upon me to reconcile, but to relate them, leaving your lordship to decide it in favour of that part which you shall judge most reasonable. And after that, in my Advertisement to the Reader, I said this : The drift 30 of the ensuing discourse is chiefly to vindicate the honour of our English writers from the censure of

those who unjustly prefer the French before them.
This I intimate, lest any should think me so exceeding
vain, as to teach others an art which they understand
much better than myself[n]. But this is more than
5 necessary to clear my modesty in that point; and I
am very confident that there is scarce any man who
has lost so much time as to read that trifle, but will
be my compurgator as to that arrogance whereof
I am accused. The truth is, if I had been naturally
10 guilty of so much vanity as to dictate my opinions,
yet I do not find that the character of a positive or
self-conceited person* is of such advantage to any in
this age, that I should labour to be publickly admitted
of that order.

15 But I am not now to defend my own cause, when
that of all the ancients and moderns is in question:
for this gentleman, who accuses me of arrogance, has
taken a course not to be taxed with the other extream
of modesty. Those propositions which are laid down
20 in my discourse, as helps to the better imitation of
nature, are not mine, (as I have said,) nor were ever
pretended so to be, but derived from the authority
of Aristotle and Horace, and from the rules and
examples of Ben Johnson and Corneille. These are
25 the men with whom properly he contends, and against

---

*Sir Robert Howard's own character. He is supposed to have
been ridiculed under the character of Sir *Positive Atall*, in Shadwell's *Sullen Lovers*, represented and published in the same year in
which this piece was written. (Malone.) Sir Positive is, adds
Scott, 'a foolish knight that pretends to understand everything in
the world, and will suffer no man to understand anything in his
company; so foolishly positive that he will never be convinced of
an error, though ever so gross.'

*whom he will endeavour to make it evident, that there is
no such thing as what they all pretend.*

His argument against the unities of place and time,
is this : *That it is as impossible for one stage to present
two rooms or houses truly, as two countries or king-* 5
*doms ; and as impossible that five hours or twenty-four
hours should be two hours, as that a thousand hours or
years should be less than what they are, or the greatest
part of time to be comprehended in the less : for all of
them being impossible, they are none of them nearest the* 10
*truth or nature of what they present ; for impossibilities
are all equal, and admit of no degree.*

This argument is so scattered into parts, that it can
scarce be united into a syllogism ; yet, in obedience
to him, *I will abbreviate* and comprehend as much of 15
it as I can in few words, that my answer to it may be
more perspicuous. I conceive his meaning to be what
follows, as to the unity of place : (if I mistake, I beg
his pardon, professing it is not out of any design
to play the *Argumentative Poet.*) If one stage cannot 20
properly present two rooms or houses, much less two
countries or kingdoms, then there can be no unity
of place ; but one stage cannot properly perform this :
therefore there can be no unity of place.

I plainly deny his minor proposition ; the force of 25
which, if I mistake not, depends on this ; that the
stage being one place cannot be two. This, indeed,
is as great a secret, as that we are all mortal*; but

---

* There is here, I believe, a covert allusion to the character in
Shadwell's play already mentioned, who in the first scene, addressing
Sandford, says, '—betwixt you and I, let me tell you, *we are all
mortal* ;' in which *wise* remark the author probably had in view
Sir Robert Howard's poem 'Against the Fear of Death.' (Malone.)

to requite it with another, I must crave leave to tell him, that though the stage cannot be two places, yet it may properly represent them, successively, or at several times. His argument is indeed no more than
5 a mere fallacy, which will evidently appear, when we distinguish place, as it relates to plays, into real and imaginary. The real place is that theatre, or piece of ground, on which the play is acted. The imaginary, that house, town, or country, where the action of the
10 *Drama* is supposed to be ; or more plainly, where the scene of the play is laid. Let us now apply this to that Herculean argument, *which, if strictly and duly weighed, is to make it evident, that there is no such thing as what they all pretend.* It is impossible, he
15 says, for one stage to present two rooms or houses : I answer, it is neither impossible, nor improper, for one real place to represent two or more imaginary places, so it be done successively ; which in other words is no more than this ; That the imagination of
20 the audience, aided by the words of the poet, and painted scenes, may suppose the stage to be some-times one place, sometimes another ; now a garden, or wood, and immediately a camp : which, I appeal to every man's imagination, if it be not true. Neither
25 the ancients nor moderns, as much fools as he is pleased to think them, ever asserted that they could make one place two ; but they might hope, by the good leave of this author, that the change of a scene might lead the imagination to suppose the place
30 altered : So that he cannot fasten those absurdities upon this scene of a play, or imaginary place of action, that it is one place, and yet two. And this

being so clearly proved, that it is past any shew of
a reasonable denial, it will not be hard to destroy
that other part of his argument which depends upon
it; namely, that it is as impossible for a stage to
represent two rooms or houses, as two countries or 5
kingdoms; for his reason is already overthrown,
which was, because both were alike impossible. This
is manifestly otherwise; for it is proved that a stage
may properly represent two rooms or houses; for
the imagination being judge òf what is represented, 10
will in reason be less chocqu'd[1] with the appearance
of two rooms in the same house, or two houses in
the same city, than with two distant cities in the
same country, or two remote countries in the same
universe. Imagination in a man or reasonable 15
creature is supposed to participate of reason; and
when that governs, as it does in the belief of fiction,
reason is not destroyed, but misled, or blinded : that
can prescribe to the reason, during the time of the
representation, somewhat like a weak belief of what 20
it sees and hears; and reason suffers itself to be so
hood-winked, that it may better enjoy the pleasures
of the fiction : but it is never so wholly made a cap-
tive, as to be drawn headlong into a perswasion of
those things which are most remote from probability: 25
'tis in that case a free-born subject, not a slave; it
will contribute willingly its assent, as far as it sees
convenient, but will not be forced. Now there is
a greater vicinity in nature betwixt two rooms than
betwixt two houses, betwixt two houses than betwixt 30

---

[1] Malone and Scott read ' choked.'

two cities, and so of the rest; Reason therefore can
sooner be led by Imagination to step from one room
into another, than to walk to two distant houses, and
yet rather to go thither, than to flye like a witch
5 through the air, and be hurried from one region to
another. Fancy and Reason go hand in hand; the
first cannot leave the last behind; and though Fancy,
when it sees the wide gulph, would venture over as
the nimbler, yet it is withheld by Reason, which will
10 refuse to take the leap, when the distance over it
appears too large. If Ben Johnson himself will remove the scene from Rome into Tuscany in the same
act, and from thence return to Rome, in the scene
which immediately follows, Reason will consider
15 there is no proportionable allowance of time to perform the journey, and therefore will chuse to stay at
home. So then, the less change of place there is,
the less time is taken up in transporting the persons
of the drama, with analogy to reason; and in that
20 analogy, or resemblance of fiction to truth, consists
the excellency of the play.

For what else concerns the unity of place, I have
already given my opinion of it in my *Essay*;—that
there is a latitude to be allowed to it,—as several
25 places in the same town or city, or places adjacent
to each other in the same country, which may all be
comprehended under the larger denomination of one
place; yet with this restriction, that the nearer and
fewer those imaginary places are, the greater re-
30 semblance they will have to truth; and reason, which
cannot make them one, will be more easily led to
suppose them so.

What has been said of the unity of place, may easily be applied to that of time : I grant it to be impossible, that the greater part of time should be comprehended in the less, that twenty-four hours should be crowded into three : but there is no necessity of that supposition. For as *Place*, so *Time* relating to a play, is either imaginary or real : the real is comprehended in those three hours, more or less, in the space of which the play is represented ; the imaginary is that which is supposed to be taken up in the representation, as twenty-four hours more or less. Now no man ever could suppose that twenty-four real hours could be included in the space of three : but where is the absurdity of affirming that the feigned business of twenty-four imagined hours may not more naturally be represented in the compass of three real hours, than the like feigned business of twenty-four years in the same proportion of real time ? For the proportions are always real, and much nearer, by his permission, of twenty-four to three, than of four thousand to it.

I am almost fearful of illustrating any thing by similitude, lest he should confute it for an argument ; yet I think the comparison of a glass will discover very aptly the fallacy of his argument, both concerning time and place. The strength of his reason depends on this, That the less cannot comprehend the greater. I have already answered, that we need not suppose it does : I say not that the less can comprehend the greater, but only that it may represent it : as in a glass or Mirrour of half a yard diameter, a whole room and many persons in it may be seen at once ; not that it can comprehend that room or those persons, but that it represents them to the sight.

5   But the author of *The Duke of Lerma* is to be excused for his declaring against the unity of time ; for, if I be not much mistaken, he is an interested person ; the time of that play taking up so many years as the favour of the Duke of Lerma continued ; nay, the
10 second and third act including all the time of his prosperity, which was a great part of the reign of Philip the Third : for in the beginning of the second act he was not yet a favourite, and before the end of the third was in disgrace. I say not this with the
15 least design of limiting the stage too servilely to twenty-four hours, however he be pleased to tax me with dogmatizing in that point. In my dialogue, as I before hinted, several persons maintained their several opinions : one of them, indeed, who sup-
20 ported the cause of the French poesie, said, how strict they were in that particular ; but he who answered in behalf of our nation, was willing to give more latitude to the rule ; and cites the words of Corneille himself, complaining against the severity
25 of it, and observing what beauties it banished from the Stage *. In few words, my own opinion is this, (and I willingly submit it to my adversary, when he will please impartially to consider it,) that the imaginary time of every play ought to be contrived into
30 as narrow a compass as the nature of the plot, the quality of the persons, and variety of accidents will

* See p. 62.

allow. In comedy I would not exceed twenty-four
or thirty hours : for the plot, accidents, and persons
of comedy are small, and may be naturally turned in
a little compass : But in tragedy the design is weighty,
and the persons great ; therefore there will naturally 5
be required a greater space of time in which to move
them. And this though Ben Johnson has not told
us, yet it is manifestly his opinion : for you see that
to his comedies he allows generally but twenty-four
hours ; to his two tragedies, *Sejanus* and *Catiline,* a 10
much larger time : though he-draws both of them into
as narrow a compass as he can : For he shews you
only the latter end of Sejanus his favour, and the
conspiracy of Catiline already ripe, and just breaking
out into action. 15

But as it is an errour on the one side, to make too
great a disproportion betwixt the imaginary time of
the play, and the real time of its representation ; so
on the other side, it is an over-sight to compress the
accidents of a play into a narrower compass than that 20
in which they could naturally be produced. Of this
last errour the French are seldom guilty, because
the thinness of their plots prevents them from it ;
but few Englishmen, except Ben Johnson, have ever
made a plot with variety of design in it, included in 25
twenty-four hours, which was altogether natural. For
this reason, I prefer *The Silent Woman* before all
other plays, I think justly ; as I do its author, in judgment, above all other poets. Yet of the two, I think
that errour the most pardonable, which in too straight 30
a compass crowds together many accidents ; since
it produces more variety, and consequently more

pleasure to the audience ; and because the nearness of proportion betwixt the imaginary and real time, does speciously cover the compression of the accidents.

Thus I have endeavoured to answer the meaning 5 of his argument ; for as he drew it, I humbly conceive that it was none ; as will appear by his proposition, and the proof of it.   His proposition was this.

If strictly and duly .weighed, it is as impossible for one stage to present two rooms or houses, as two coun- 10 *tries or kingdoms,* &c.   And his proof this : *For all being impossible, they are none of them nearest the truth or nature of what they present.*

Here you see, instead of proof or reason, there is only *petitio principii* : for in plain words, his sense is 15 this ; Two things are as impossible as one another, because they are both equally impossible : but he takes those two things to be granted as impossible which he ought to have proved such, before he had proceeded to prove them equally impossible : he should 20 have made out first, that it was impossible for one stage to represent two houses, and then have gone forward to prove that it was as equally impossible for a stage to present two houses, as two countries.

After all this, the very absurdity to which he would 25 reduce mè is none at all : for he only drives at this, That if his argument be true, I must then acknowledge that there are degrees in impossibilities, which I easily grant him without dispute : and if I mistake not, Aristotle and the School are of my opinion.   For 30 there are some things which are absolutely impossible, and others which are only so *ex parte* ; as it is absolutely impossible for a thing *to be,* and *not be,* at

the same time ; but for a stone to move naturally up-
ward, is only impossible *ex parte materiæ* ; but it is not
impossible for the first mover to alter the nature of it.

His last assault, like that of a Frenchman, is most
feeble : for whereas I have observed, that none have 5
been violent against verse, but such only as have not
attempted it, or have succeeded ill in their attempt,
he will needs, according to his usual custom, improve
my observation to an argument, that he might have
the glory to confute it. But I lày my observation at 10
his feet, as I do my pen, which I have often employed
willingly in his deserved commendations, and now
most unwillingly against his judgment. For his
person and parts, I honour them as much as any
man living, and have had so many particular obliga- 15
tions to him, that I should be very ungrateful, if I did
not acknowledge them to the world. But I gave not
the first occasion of this difference in opinions. In
my Epistle Dedicatory before my *Rival Ladies*, I had
said somewhat in behalf of verse, which he was pleased 20
to answer in his Preface to his plays : that occasioned
my reply in my Essay ; and that reply begot this re-
joynder of his in his Preface to *The Duke of Lerma*.
But as I was the last who took up arms, I will be the
first to lay them down. For what I have here written, 25
I submit it wholly to him ; and if I do not hereafter
answer what may be objected against this paper, I
hope the world will not impute it to any other reason,
than only the due respect which I have for so noble
an opponent. 30

NOTES.

Page 1. Charles Sackville, Lord Buckhurst, afterwards
Earl of Dorset, author of the well-known song 'To all you
ladies now on land,' and Lord Chamberlain to William III
after the Revolution, was always a kind friend and patron to
Dryden, and liberally assisted him when the loss of his office
as poet-laureat, through his refusal to take the oaths to
William, brought the poet to great distress. See the long
dedication to Dryden's *Essay on Satire* (Yonge's edition).

2. l. 17. *The Tragedy of Pompey the Great*, ' translated out
of French by certain persons of honour': 4to. 1664. From
Dryden's eulogium it appears that the fourth act was translated by Lord Buckhurst; the first was done by Waller.
(Malone.) Sir Charles Sedley, Malone says in another place,
had also a hand in this translation, which was from the
Pompée of Corneille. The act translated by Waller is
published among his works.

3. 6. See Valerius Maximus, l. iv. c. 5. (Malone.)

8. Hor. Epod. xvi. 37.

13. To *allow*, in the last age, signified to approve. (Malone.)

3. 27. I have not, any more than former editors, succeeded
in discovering from what French poet these lines are taken.

4. 13. These lines are found in a poem by Sir William
Davenant, printed in 4to. in 1663, and republished in his
works, fol. 1673, p. 268. (Malone.)

28. In the Dedication to *The Rival Ladies* [1664]
(Malone); where Dryden argues very ably for the superiority
of rhyme over blank verse.

5. 18. See Cicero's Letters to Atticus, xii. 40, and Plutarch's
Life of Julius Caesar, chap. 54.

7. 5. Dryden often uses adjectives as adverbs. In this

K

particular instance he had Shakspere's example before him. See *Henry VIII*, iv. 2. 52 :—

> 'Exceeding wise, fair-spoken. and persuading.'

8. 15. The engagement between the English and Dutch fleets took place [off Southwold] in Suffolk. In this memorable battle 18 large Dutch ships were taken, and 14 others were destroyed ; Opdam, the Dutch admiral, who engaged the Duke of York, was blown up beside him, and he and all his crew perished. (Malone.)

11. 5. This is probably a reference to the Act of 1664, commonly called the Conventicle Act, 'to prevent and suppress seditious and unlawful conventicles.'

16. Cic. *pro Archia*, c. 10.

21. Perhaps the writer first alluded to was Dr. Robert Wild, author of *Iter Boreale*, a panegyric on General Monk, published in April 1660, and often reprinted ; which may be the 'famous poem' alluded to in p. 13. His works were collected and published in a small volume in 1668. The other poet may have been Richard Flecknoe. Both these poets celebrated the Dutch defeat. (Malone.)

13. 2. Martial. Epigr. viii. 19.

13. 23. George Wither, probably because he was a Puritan and one of Cromwell's major-generals, was the mark for much malicious satire on the part of Tory and Royalist poets. They give him no credit for the lovely lyrical pieces which are for ever associated with his name. Butler (*Hudibras*, Part I, canto 1), addressing the Puritanic muse, says :—

> 'Thou that with ale, or viler liquors,
> Didst inspire Withers, Prynne, and Vickars.'

Dryden speaks contemptuously of him in the passage before us, and Pope in the *Dunciad* (i. 296) numbers 'wretched Withers' among 'the dull of ancient days.'

30. 'Auction by inch of Candle, is when, a piece of candle being lighted, people are allowed to bid while it burns, but as soon as extinct, the commodity is adjudged to the last bidder.' (Chambers' Dictionary.) At land sales in France this practice is still in force.

14. 17. T. Petronius, *Satyricon*, cap. ii.

15. 6. Hor. *Epist.* ii. 1. 76.

9. *Ib.* 34.

16. 21. Malone rejects 'Eugenius his opinion' as 'un-grammatical phraseology,' but says, supporting himself on the authority of Bishop Lloyd, that Dryden ought to have written 'Eugeniusis opinion'!

17. 26. It is not perfect, because it does not include a *differentia*, and is therefore too wide; it is applicable to epic and heroic poems, and to romances, equally with plays.

18. 11. See Vell. Paterc. i. 16. 17. (Malone.)

19. 14. *Historia Romana*, i. 17.

20. 22. Aristotle's treatise ón Poetry 'is a fragment, and while promising to treat of tragedy, comedy, and epic poetry, it treats only of tragedy, adding a few brief remarks on epic poetry, and omitting comedy altogether.' (Encyc. Brit. 9th ed., art. 'Aristotle.')

23. 18. Ben Jonson's *Discoveries*, p. 765 of Routledge's edition of his Works.

27. 9. *Historia Romana*, ii. 92.

28. 23. Horace's line is :—

'Neve minor, neu sit quinto productior actu.'

(Malone.) *Ars Poet.* 189. Horace lays it down as a rule applicable to all plays, not comedies only.

29. The term 'Jornada' was introduced into Spain by the dramatist Naharro early in the sixteenth century. It is equivalent to day's work, or day's journey. 'The old French mysteries were divided into *journées* or portions, each of which could conveniently be represented in the time given by the Church to such entertainments on a single day. One of the mysteries in this way required forty days for its exhibition.' (Ticknor, *Spanish Literature*, i. 270 *note*.)

29. 7. τὸ μῦθος. This is a singular slip; it should of course be ὁ μῦθος.

28. 'Good cheap' is a literal translation of *bon marché*.

31. 24. The *Supplices*.

34. 14. The satyric drama of the *Cyclops*, by Euripides, a

K 2

kind of farce, is the only specimen remaining to us of a form
of theatrical entertainment which all the Greek tragedians
had recourse to, in order to relieve the mental tension con-
sequent on witnessing the performance of a long tragedy.
It must be remembered, however, that with them a tragedy
was merely a drama written in an intense and serious style;
it was not necessary that it should have a disastrous ending.
Thus the *Alcestis*, the *Ion*, and the two *Iphigenias* of
Euripides, and the *Electra* and *Œdipus Coloneus* of Sophocles,
since none of these plays end unhappily, do not fall under
the definition of a tragedy as now understood.

35. 6. Ter. *Eunuchus*, Act. ii. Sc. I. 17, 18.

16. Our author has quoted from memory. The lines
are, *At nostri proavi*, etc., and afterwards, *Ne dicam* stulte
mirati. (Malone.) Hor. *A. P.* 270.

23. Hor. *A. P.* 70.

28. Catachresis is the improper or abusive employment
of a word.

29. Virg. *Ecl.* iv. 20.

36. 4. Virg. *Æn.* viii. 91.

8. Ovid, *Met.* i. 175; and (below) *ib.* 561. Malone says
that the true reading is *pompae*, and this is certainly adopted
in Burmann's edition; but *longas ... pompas* occurs in some
MSS. Malone also points out that in the preceding quotation, for *verbo* we should read *verbis*, and for *metuam summi*,
timeam magni.

31. From *The Rebel Scot*, by Cleveland.

37. I. Juv. *Sat.* x. 123.

22. Many Medeas were produced by the ancients;
Delrio tells us that it was treated as a subject for comedy by
the Greek authors, Eubulus, Stratis, and Cantharus, and for
tragedy by (besides Euripides) Herillus, Diogenes, Philiscus,
and Demologus; it was also dramatized by the Latin writers
Ennius, Attius, Pacuvius, Varro, and Ovid. (See Schröder's
Seneca; Delft, 1728.)

25. Ovid, *Tristia* ii. 381.

30. Our author (as Dr. Johnson has observed) might
have determined this question upon surer evidence, for it

[*Medea*] is quoted by Quintilian as Seneca's, and the only line which remains of Ovid's play, for one line is left us, is not found there. (Malone.) Ovid's line, cited by Quintilian in his eighth book, as stronger and more impressive than the adage *Nocere facile est, prodesse difficile,* is — *Servare potui. Perdere an possim rogas?*

38. 20. Juv. *Sat.* vi. 195.

39. 17. Virg. *Æn.* i. 378; parts of two lines.

28. Hor. *Sat.* x. 68.

41. 10. Pierre Corneille was born at Rouen in 1606, and produced his first play, *Mélite,* a comedy, in 1625.

42. 28. The Red Bull, in St. John's Street, was one of the meanest of our ancient theatres, and was famous for entertainments adapted to the taste of the lower orders of the people. (Malone.) In Strype's edition of Stow's *London* there is a plan of the parish of St. James, Clerkenwell, on which is marked 'Red Bull Yard,' between St. John's Street and Clerkenwell Green. This must have been the site of the theatre. The ground formerly belonged to the priory of St. John at Jerusalem; and it is not unlikely that, as Shakspeare and his company turned the ruinous buildings of the Blackfriars, near St. Paul's, to account for a theatre, the patrons of the Red Bull made a similar use of the monastic ruins at Clerkenwell. In his *Annals of the Stage* (iii. 324) Mr. Collier collects a number of notices, more or less interesting, of the Red Bull Theatre. Wither, in his satires, Randolph in his *Muses' Looking Glass,* and Prynne in the *Histriomastix,* all make mention of it. It was pulled down not long after the Restoration, and Drury Lane was regarded as having taken its place.

29. Hor. *Epist.* ii. 1. 185. Horace wrote:—

'Si discordet eques, media inter carmina poscunt
Aut ursum aut pugiles.'

43. 13. *Ars Poet.* 240.

22. *Ib.* 151.

28. Dryden here used 'success' in the sense of the Spanish *suceso,* which means 'event,' or 'issue.'

44. 3. The writers from whom we learn the story of Cyrus are Herodotus, Ctesias, and Xenophon. Of these Herodotus, as living nearest to the time, is the most trustworthy. The *Cyropaedia* of Xenophon is a historical romance, nor does the writer himself pretend that it is anything more. Herodotus makes Cyrus, when advanced in years, invade the country of the Massagetae, whose queen was Tomyris, and lose his life in battle. (Smith's Class. Biogr. Dictionary.)

21. Hor. *de Arte Poet.* 188.

25. Hesiod, *Theog.* 27.

45. 15. *The Bloody Brother*, also called *The Tragedy of Rollo Duke of Normandy*, by John Fletcher, was first printed in 1639. The plot is taken from the fourth book of Herodian; it is Roman imperial history transferred to new times, places, and persons; Caracalla and Geta become Rollo and Otto. Whatever merit the piece may have in respect of uniformity, the versification and style are both of a low and rude type.

26. *Oleo*, or *oglio*, is a corruption of *olla* in *olla podrida*, a Spanish dish consisting of a stew of several kinds of meat and vegetables. *Oleo*, therefore, means a mess or mixture.

47. 3. Dryden appears to have borrowed this word from Corneille, who speaks (*Rodog.* Exam.) of a 'personage protatique,' i.e. an introductory character; it is from the Greek προτατικός.

50. 13. Hor. *A. P.* 180–187. Horace writes ' *Ne* pueros': a line is omitted after 'trucidet.'

25. The reference is to Act iii, Sc. i. 2, of Jonson's comedy of *The Magnetic Lady*.

51. 9. The title of this play, the joint work of Beaumont and Fletcher, and first acted in 1611, was *A King and no King*. In the last act Gobryas, a noble, reveals to Arbaces, king of Illyria, that he is really his son, and not the son of Arane, the queen mother; Arbaces, thus become a subject and 'no King,' marries Panthea, the true heir to the throne, and all ends happily.

52. 2. *The Scornful Lady*, a joint play, was produced some time between 1609 and 1615. 'The sudden conversion of the usurer Morecraft is imitated from the *Adelphi* of

Terence, where the same change takes place in the character of Demea.' (Dyce.)

53. 19. Velleius Paterculus, i. 17. (Malone.)

54. 17. The *Menteur* of Corneille (see Geruzez, *Lit. Française*, ii. 90) was founded on one of the *chefs d'œuvre* of the Spanish stage, the *Truth itself Suspected* of Ruiz de Alarcon. It appeared in 1642.

23. It seems impossible to compare such plays as the *Menteur* and the *Fox* of Jonson. The latter is real life, though in a coarse form ; the other, with its polished rhymes and regular movement, is a fine work of art, but has little to do with life. Each has its merits, but they are referable to no common standard.

55. 5. Cardinal Richelieu died in 1642. (Malone.)

9. The *Cornelia* and *Double Marriage* of Beaumont and Fletcher, which are founded on two of Cervantes' novels, are cases in point.

11. *The Adventures of Five Hours*, written by Sir Samuel Tuke, and printed in 1663. Diego is a character in it. (Malone.)

56. l. 6. 'Contraries are the two most opposite qualities of the same class of subjects, *e.g.* black and white, as colours of bodies ; virtue and vice, as habits of the soul.' (Mansel's *Artis Logicae Rudimenta*, 19.)

57. 4. The doctrine of the *primum mobile* belongs to the Ptolemaic astronomy, which made the sun and stars revolve round the earth.

58. 12. *Cinna, or the Clemency of Augustus*, produced in 1639, is generally allowed to be Corneille's finest tragedy. On the *Pompey*, see the note on p. 129. The *Polyeuctus*, a story of Christian martyrdom referring to the persecution of the Emperor Decius, appeared in 1640. The author's 'Examen' on this play is of great interest.

60. 10. *The Maid's Tragedy* is by Beaumont and Fletcher ; the other plays here mentioned, by Ben Jonson.

61. 16. The *Andromède,* from the gorgeousness of its mythological *mise-en-scène*, bore some resemblance to the masque, while from the use of recitative and the introduction of many songs it approached the modern opera. Among the 'dramatis personae' there were only ten human beings against twelve gods and goddesses. The opening scene showed a huge mountain, pierced by a grotto, through which appeared the sea ; Melpomene entered on one side, and the Sun on the other, in a 'char tout lumineux,' drawn by four horses.

62. 9. There is no passage in Ben Jonson's works in which he directly censures Shakspere for the non-observance of the unities of Time and Place. Dryden can only refer to the Prologue to *Every Man in his Humour.* This prologue first appeared in 1616, and its intended application to Shakspere may well have been traditionally known in the theatrical world fifty years later. In it Jonson, among the 'ill customs of the age' which he will not imitate, enumerates—

> 'To make a child now swaddled to proceed
> Man, and then shoot up, in one beard and weed,
> Past threescore years ; or, with three rusty swords,
> And help of some few foot and half-foot words,
> Fight over York and Lancaster's long jars,
> And in the tyring-house bring wounds to scars.
> He rather prays you will be pleased to see
> One such to-day, as other plays should be ;
> Where neither chorus wafts you o'er the seas,
> Nor creaking throne comes down the boys to please,' etc.

Other dramatists may have been included in the censure ; but it seems clear that Shakspere was principally intended, the three parts of whose *Henry VI* extend over the events of nearly fifty years, including the whole of 'York and Lancaster's long jars,' whose Perdita is born and grows up to be a woman between the first and fifth acts, and who makes the Chorus in *Winter's Tale* say—the play having begun in Sici.y—

> 'imagine me,
> Gentle spectators, that I now may be
> In fair Bohemia.'

64. 19. A servant in Sir Samuel Tuke's *Adventures of Five Hours*, who is described by the author as 'a great coward, and a pleasant droll.' Philipin is, I suppose, a character in the French play alluded to. (Malone.)

65. 23. This subject had been imperfectly examined at the time when Dryden wrote, and his statement is not quite accurate. It is true that most of the old comedies before Shakspere, such as *Ralph Roister Doister* and *Gammer Gurton's Needle,* were written in rude twelve-syllable lines, to class which with the elegant French Alexandrines of the period is to pay them much too high a compliment. But there were exceptions; the *Misogonus* of Richards (about 1560) is in fourteen-syllable alternate rhymes; the *Supposes* of Gascoigne (1566) is in prose; the *Promos and Cassandra* of Whetstone (1578) is in the heroic couplet; and the *Taming of a Shrew* (1594) is in blank verse. See Collier, *Annals of the Stage,* vol. iii.

30. The unfinished pastoral drama of *The Sad Shepherd, or A Tale of Robin Hood,* must have been written not long before Jonson's death in 1637; the prologue opens with the line—

' He that hath feasted you *these forty years.*'

66. 3. The pastoral drama of *The Faithful Shepherdess,* by Fletcher, was brought out about 1610.

18. Dryden truly says that *The Merry Wives of Windsor* is ' almost exactly formed '; that is, that the unities of time and place are nearly observed. The time of the action is comprised within two days; the place is, either some house in Windsor, or a street in Windsor, or a field near the town, or Windsor Park.

67. 11. It is curious to observe with what caution our author speaks, when he ventures to place Shakspere above Jonson; a caution which proves decisively the wretched taste of the period when he wrote. (Malone.)

31. Virg. *Ecl.* i. 26.

68. 23. Chiefly on account of the woman-page Bellario, in whose mouth are put a profusion of pretty and graceful things which might often deserve to have been said by Shakspere's Viola. Lamb says (*Eng. Dramatic Poets,* p. 308), ' For many years after the date of *Philaster's* first exhibition on the stage [1608], scarce a play can be found without one of these women pages in it, following in the train of some pre-engaged lover.'

69. 10. Mr. Dyce, in his excellent edition of Beaumont and Fletcher (1844), enumerates the following plays as certainly, or almost certainly, the joint work of the two :—

Philaster.
The Maid's Tragedy.
The Knight of the Burning Pestle.
King and no King.
Cupid's Revenge.
The Coxcomb.
Four Plays in One.
The Scornful Lady.
The Honest Man's Fortune.
The Little French Lawyer.
Wit at several Weapons.
The Laws of Candy.

Three others—*Wit without Money, The Custom of the Country*, and *Bonduca*—he is disposed to add to the above list, but with less confidence. The other plays, in number about thirty-nine, published under their joint names, he would assign either to Fletcher alone, or to Fletcher assisted by some other dramatist, not Beaumont.

71. 9. The *Discoveries*, not published till after Jonson's death, are like the contents of a commonplace book, and of very unequal merit ; here occurs the well-known criticism on Shakspere as having 'never blotted out a line.' The praise which Dryden gives to the book is excessive. To go no further, the 'Examens' annexed by Corneille to his dramas are incomparably more valuable than anything in the *Discoveries*.

13. *Epicœne, or the Silent Woman*, appeared in 1609.

73. 14. τὸ γελοῖον (to geloion), the laughable or ridiculous element.

26. ἦθος, disposition ; πάθος, passion (ēthos, pathos).

75. 25. Hor. *Epist.* ii. 1. 168.

76. 19. The prose comedy of *Bartholomew Fair* was produced in 1614.

77. 17. Of the piece on which our author has given so high

an encomium, Drummond of Hawthornden, Jonson's con-
temporary and friend, has left the following anecdote : ' When
his play of *The Silent Woman* was first acted, there were
found verses after on the stage against him, concluding that
the play was well named *The Silent Woman*, because there
was never one man to say *plaudite* to it.' (Malone.)

78. 18. Hor. *de Arte Poet.* 90.

25. Vell. Paterc. ii. 36.

80. 13. Macrob. *Saturnalia*, ii. 13. The ' other poet ' was
Publius Syrus.

81. 1. Aristotle's *Poetics*, iv. 18.

24. Virg. *Ecl.* vii. 4.

83. 9. M. Seneca, *Controv.* ix. 5, quoting from Ovid, *Met.*
xiii. 503–5.

11. Ovid, *Met.* i. 292. This line is quoted by Lucius,
not by Marcus Seneca.

29. *The Indian Queen* and *The Indian Emperor* were
the only plays, altogether in rhyme, which Dryden had produced before this was written. *The Rival Ladies* is partly
prose, partly rhyme.

84. 3. Sir Robert Howard (Malone) ; in the preface to his
plays, published in 1665.

85. 29. ' prevail himself,' *se prévaloir*, a Gallicism.

87. 10. ' Vide Daniel, his Defence of Rhyme.' (Dryden's
note.) This short tract was written by Daniel in 1603, in reply
to Campion's *Observations in the Art of English Poesie.*

88. 4. *The Siege of Rhodes* (1656) was one of the plays
produced by Sir William Davenant under the Protectorate ;
' a kind of nondescript *entertainments*, as they were called,
which were dramatic in everything but the names and form ;
and some of them were called operas.' (Hazlitt.)

90. 3. Virg. *Georg.* iii. 9 ; for *possum* should be read *possim.*

19. Geo. Sandys, son of an archbishop of York, published
a metrical version of the Psalms in 1636.

90. 24. Our author here again has quoted from memory.
Horace's line is [Epist. ii. 1. 63] :—

' Interdum vulgus rectum videt ; est ubi peccat.'
(Malone.)

30. *Mustapha* was a popular tragedy of the day, by Roger Boyle, Earl of Orrery. There was an earlier play of the same name by Fulke Greville, afterwards Lord Brooke.

91. 27. Hor. *A. P.* 90 ; and below, *ib.* 231.

95. 11. This simple avowal of the true poetic workman, that his work does not appear to him perfect till he has clothed it in rhyme, is highly instructive ; it is a chapter in the ' Natural History of Poetry.'

96. 2. The Water-poet, John Taylor, was so called from his having been long a waterman on the Thames. He seems to have been a rhymester of the same order as ' Poet Close,' a character well known to all who visit Windermere. Wood gives an account of him in the *Athenae*, and Hazlitt devotes rather a lengthy article to him in his edition of Johnson's *Lives*. Taylor enjoyed a great popularity. ' If it were put to the question,' says Ben Jonson (*Discoveries*, Routledge, p. 746), ' of the water-rhymer's works against Spenser's, I doubt not but they would find more suffrages ; because the most favour common vices, out of a prerogative the vulgar have to lose their judgments, and like that which is naught.'

7. Cicero in his *Brutus* (cap. 73) quotes this as a maxim laid down by Caesar in his work ' on the method of speaking in Latin,' to which the name ' De Analogia ' was given.

13. Seneca's tragedy of *Hippolytus*, l. 863.

97. 28. Sir Robert Howard, in the Preface to his Plays, before referred to.

99. 22. ' Somerset House,' says Stow in his *History of London* (ed. Strype, 1720), ' hath been used as the Palace or Court of the Queen Dowagers ; it belong'd of late to Katharine Queen Dowager, the wife of King Charles the Second. At the entrance into this Court out of the Strand is a spacious square court garnished on all sides with rows of freestone buildings, and at the Front is a *Piazza*, with stone Pillars which support the buildings, and a pavement of freestone.' He goes on to say that there were steps down to the river, and a ' most pleasant garden which runs to the water side.' This way from the river bank up into Somerset House has long been closed.

105. 28. Hor. *A. P.* 362.

30. *Ib.* 50.

108. 10. 'lazar' sometimes='lazar-house'; and the reference seems to be to Bartholomew's Hospital, which is the scene of the play of *Bartholomew Fair.*

111. 9. Lucan, *Phars.* i. 12.

114. 3. Hor. *de Art. Poet.* 338.

115. 5. *Il.* viii. 267.

118. 4. See above, pp. 6 and 8.

THE END

Clarendon Press Series.

The English Language and Literature.

HELPS TO THE STUDY OF THE LANGUAGE.

1. DICTIONARIES.

A NEW ENGLISH DICTIONARY, ON HISTORICAL PRIN-CIPLES: founded mainly on the materials collected by the Philological Society. Imperial 4to.

PRESENT STATE OF THE WORK.

			£	s.	d.
Vol. I. {A B} Edited by Dr. MURRAY. . . . . Half-morocco			2	12	6
Vol. II. C Edited by Dr. MURRAY. . . . . Half-morocco			2	12	6
Vol. III. { D Edited by Dr. MURRAY .	D–Depravation . . .		o	8	6
	Depravative-Development		o	2	6
	Development-Diffluency		o	2	6
	Diffluent-Disburden . .		o	2	6
	Disburdened-Disobservant		o	2	6
E Edited by HENRY BRADLEY	{ E-Every . .		o	12	6
	Everybody-Ezod .		o	5	0
Vol. IV. { F Edited by HENRY BRADLEY	{ F-Field . .		o	7	6
	Field-Fish . .		o	2	6
	Fish-Flexuose .		o	2	6
G To be edited by HENRY BRADLEY. *In Preparation.*					

.*.* One Section at least, consisting of Sixty-four Pages, is now published Quarterly at Half-a-Crown.

Bosworth and **Toller.** *An Anglo-Saxon Dictionary*, based on the MS. Collections of the late JOSEPH BOSWORTH, D.D. Edited and enlarged by Prof. T. N. TOLLER, M.A. Parts I-III, A-SAR. . . . [4to, 15s. each. Part IV, Section I, SAR—SWÍÐRIAN. . . . . [4to, 8s. 6d.

Mayhew and **Skeat.** *A Concise Dictionary of Middle English*, from A. D. 1150 to 1580. By A. L. MAYHEW, M.A., and W. W. SKEAT, Litt.D. [Crown 8vo, half-roan, 7s. 6d.

Skeat. *A Concise Etymological Dictionary of the English Language.* By W. W. SKEAT, Litt.D. *Sixth Edition.* . . [Crown 8vo, 5s. 6d.

2. GRAMMARS, READING BOOKS, &c.

Earle. *The Philology of the English Tongue.* By J. EARLE, M.A., Professor of Anglo-Saxon. *Fifth Edition.* . . [Extra fcap. 8vo, 8s. 6d.

—— *A Book for the Beginner in Anglo-Saxon.* By J. EARLE, M.A., Professor of Anglo-Saxon. *Third Edition.* . . [Extra fcap. 8vo, 2s. 6d.

Mayhew. *Synopsis of Old-English Phonology.* By A. L. MAYHEW, M.A. . . . . . . [Extra fcap. 8vo, bevelled boards, 8s. 6d.

Morris and **Skeat.** *Specimens of Early English—*
Part I. From Old English Homilies to King Horn (A.D. 1150 to A.D. 1300). By R. MORRIS, LL.D. *Second Edition.* . . [Extra fcap. 8vo, 9s.
Part II. From Robert of Gloucester to Gower (A.D. 1298 to A.D. 1393). By R. MORRIS, LL.D., and W. W. SKEAT, Litt.D. *Third Edition.* [7s. 6d.

Skeat. *Specimens of English Literature,* from the 'Ploughmans Crede' to the 'Shepheardes Calender.' . . [Extra fcap. 8vo, 7s. 6d.

—— *The Principles of English Etymology—*
First Series. The Native Element. *Second Edition.* [Crown 8vo, 10s. 6d.
Second Series. The Foreign Element. . . . [Crown 8vo, 10s. 6d.

—— *A Primer of English Etymology.* [Extra fcap. 8vo, *stiff covers,* 1s. 6d.

—— *Twelve Facsimiles of Old-English Manuscripts.* [4to, 7s. 6d.

Sweet. *A New English Grammar, Logical and Historical.* Part I. Introduction, Phonology, and Accidence. . . . [Crown 8vo, 10s. 6d.

—— *A Short Historical English Grammar.* [Extra fcap. 8vo, 4s. 6d.

—— *A Primer of Historical English Grammar.* [Extra fcap. 8vo, 2s.

—— *History of English Sounds from the Earliest Period.* With full Word-Lists. . . . . [8vo, 14s.

—— *An Anglo-Saxon Primer, with Grammar, Notes, and Glossary.* By HENRY SWEET, M.A. *Eighth Edition.* . . [Extra fcap. 8vo, 2s. 6d.

—— *An Anglo-Saxon Reader.* In Prose and Verse. With Grammatical Introduction, Notes, and Glossary. By the same Author. *Seventh Edition, Revised and Enlarged.* . . . . . [Crown 8vo, 9s. 6d.

—— *A Second Anglo-Saxon Reader.* By the same Author. [4s. 6d.

—— *Old English Reading Primers.* By the same Author—
I. *Selected Homilies of Ælfric.* . . [Extra fcap. 8vo, *stiff covers,* 2s.
II. *Extracts from Alfred's Orosius.* . [Extra fcap. 8vo, *stiff covers,* 2s.

—— *First Middle English Primer, with Grammar and Glossary.* By the same Author. *Second Edition.* . . . [Extra fcap. 8vo, 2s. 6d.

—— *Second Middle English Primer.* Extracts from Chaucer, with Grammar and Glossary. By the same Author. . [Extra fcap. 8vo, 2s. 6d.

—— *A Primer of Spoken English.* . . . [Extra fcap. 8vo, 3s. 6d.

—— *A Primer of Phonetics.* . . . . [Extra fcap. 8vo, 3s. 6d.

—— *A Manual of Current Shorthand, Orthographic and Phonetic.* [4s. 6d.

Tancock. *An Elementary English Grammar and Exercise Book.* By O. W. TANCOCK, M.A. *Third Edition.* . . [Extra fcap. 8vo, 1s. 6d.

—— *An English Grammar and Reading Book,* for Lower Forms in Classical Schools. By O. W. TANCOCK, M.A. *Fourth Edition.* [3s. 6d.

A SERIES OF ENGLISH CLASSICS.

(CHRONOLOGICALLY ARRANGED.)

Chaucer. I. *The Prologue to the Canterbury Tales.* (*School Edition.*) Edited by W. W. SKEAT, Litt.D. . . [Extra fcap. 8vo, *stiff covers*, 1s.

———— II. *The Prologue; The Knightes Tale; The Nonne Prestes Tale.* Edited by R. MORRIS, LL.D. *A New Edition, with Collations and Additional Notes*, by W. W. SKEAT, Litt.D. . . [Extra fcap. 8vo, 2s. 6d.

———— III. *The Prioresses Tale; Sir Thopas; The Monkes Tale; The Clerkes Tale; The Squieres Tale, &c.* Edited by W. W. SKEAT, Litt.D. *Fourth Edition.* . . . . [Extra fcap. 8vo, 4s. 6d.

———— IV. *The Tale of the Man of Lawe; The Pardoneres Tale; The Second Nonnes Tale; The Chanouns Yemannes Tale.* By the same Editor. *New Edition, Revised.* . . . . [Extra fcap. 8vo, 4s. 6d.

———— V. *Minor Poems.* By the same Editor. [Crown 8vo, 10s. 6d.

———— VI. *The Legend of Good Women.* By the same Editor. [Crown 8vo, 6s.

———— VII. *The Hous of Fame.* By the same Editor. [Crown 8vo, 2s.

Langland. *The Vision of William concerning Piers the Plowman,* by WILLIAM LANGLAND. Edited by W. W. SKEAT, Litt.D. *Sixth Edition.* [Extra fcap. 8vo, 4s. 6d.

Gamelyn, The Tale of. Edited by W. W. SKEAT, Litt.D. [Extra fcap. 8vo, *stiff covers*, 1s. 6d.

Wycliffe. *The New Testament in English,* according to the Version by JOHN WYCLIFFE, about A.D. 1380, and Revised by JOHN PURVEY, about A.D. 1388. With Introduction and Glossary by W. W. SKEAT, Litt.D. [Extra fcap. 8vo, 6s.

———— *The Books of Job, Psalms, Proverbs, Ecclesiastes, and the Song of Solomon:* according to the Wycliffite Version made by NICHOLAS DE HEREFORD, about A.D. 1381, and Revised by JOHN PURVEY, about A.D. 1388. With Introduction and Glossary by W.W.SKEAT, Litt.D. [Extra fcap. 8vo, 3s. 6d.

Minot. *The Poems of Laurence Minot.* Edited, with Introduction and Notes, by JOSEPH HALL, M.A. . . . . [Extra fcap. 8vo, 4s. 6d.

Spenser. *The Faery Queene.* Books I and II. Edited by G. W. KITCHIN, D.D., with Glossary by A. L. MAYHEW, M.A. [Extra fcap. 8vo, 2s. 6d. each.

Hooker. *Ecclesiastical Polity,* Book I. Edited by R. W. CHURCH, M.A., late Dean of St. Paul's. *Second Edition.* . . [Extra fcap. 8vo, 2s.

Marlowe and Greene. MARLOWE'S *Tragical History of Dr. Faustus,* and GREENE'S *Honourable History of Friar Bacon and Friar Bungay.* Edited by A.W.WARD, Litt.D. *New and Enlarged Edition.* [Crown 8vo, 6s. 6d.

Marlowe. *Edward II.* Edited by O. W. TANCOCK, M.A. *Second Edition.* . . . . . [Extra fcap. 8vo. *Paper covers,* 2s.; *cloth,* 3s.

Shakespeare. Select Plays. Edited by W. G. CLARK, M.A., and
W. ALDIS WRIGHT, D.C.L. . . . . [Extra fcap. 8vo, *stiff covers.*

The Merchant of Venice. 1s.	*Macbeth.* 1s. 6d.
Richard the Second. 1s. 6d.	*Hamlet.* 2s.

Edited by W. ALDIS WRIGHT, D.C.L.

The Tempest. 1s. 6d.	*Coriolanus.* 2s. 6d.
As You Like It. 1s. 6d.	*Richard the Third.* 2s. 6d.
A Midsummer Night's Dream. 1s. 6d.	*Henry the Fifth.* 2s.
Twelfth Night. 1s. 6d.	*King John.* 1s. 6d.
Julius Caesar. 2s.	*King Lear.* 1s. 6d.
Henry the Eighth. 2s.	*Much Ado About Nothing.* 1s. 6d.

Shakespeare as a Dramatic Artist; *a popular Illustration of the
Principles of Scientific Criticism.* By R. G. MOULTON, M.A. [Cr. 8vo, 7s. 6d.

Bacon. *Advancement of Learning.* Edited by W. ALDIS WRIGHT,
D.C.L. *Third Edition.* . . . . . [Extra fcap. 8vo, 4s. 6d.

——— *The Essays.* Edited, with Introduction and Illustrative Notes,
by S. H. REYNOLDS, M.A. . . . . [Demy 8vo, *half-bound*, 12s. 6d.

Milton. I. *Areopagitica.* With Introduction and Notes. By JOHN
W. HALES, M.A. *Third Edition.* . . . . [Extra fcap. 8vo, 3s.

——— II. *Poems.* Edited by R. C. BROWNE, M.A. In two
Volumes. *New Edition.* . . . . . [Extra fcap. 8vo, 6s. 6d.
. . . . Sold separately, Vol. I. 4s., Vol. II. 3s.

In paper covers: *Lycidas*, 3d. *Comus*, 6d.

By OLIVER ELTON, B.A.

Lycidas, 6d. *L'Allegro*, 4d. *Il Penseroso*, 4d. *Comus*, 1s.

——— III. *Paradise Lost.* Book I. Edited with Notes, by H. C.
BEECHING, M.A. . . [Extra fcap. 8vo, 1s. 6d. *In Parchment*, 3s. 6d.

——— IV. *Paradise Lost.* Book II. Edited by E. K. CHAMBERS,
B.A. .· . . [Extra fcap. 8vo, 1s. 6d. Books I and II together, 2s. 6d.

——— V. *Samson Agonistes.* Edited, with Introduction and Notes,
by JOHN CHURTON COLLINS, M.A. . . [Extra fcap. 8vo, *stiff covers*, 1s.

Milton's Prosody. By ROBERT BRIDGES. [Extra fcap. 8vo, 1s. 6d.

Bunyan. I. *The Pilgrim's Progress, Grace Abounding, Relation of
the Imprisonment of Mr. John Bunyan.* Edited by E. VENABLES, M.A.
[Extra fcap. 8vo, 3s. 6d. *In Parchment*, 4s. 6d.

——— II. *The Holy War, and the Heavenly Footman.* Edited by MABEL
PEACOCK. . . . . [Extra fcap. 8vo, 3s. 6d.

Clarendon. I. *History of the Rebellion.* Book VI. Edited, with Introduction and Notes, by T. ARNOLD, M.A. *Second Edition.* [Crown 8vo, 5s.

——— II. *Selections.* Edited by G. BOYLE, M.A., Dean of Salisbury.
[Crown 8vo, 7s. 6d.

Dryden. *Select Poems.* (*Stanzas on the Death of Oliver Cromwell;
Astræa Redux; Annus Mirabilis; Absalom and Achitophel; Religio Laici;
The Hind and the Panther.*) Edited by W. D. CHRISTIE, M.A. *Fifth Edition.*
Revised by C. H. FIRTH, M.A. . . . . [Extra fcap. 8vo, 3s. 6d.

——— *Essay of Dramatic Poesy.* Edited, with Notes, by T. ARNOLD,
M.A. . . . . [Extra fcap. 8vo, 3s. 6d.

Locke. *Conduct of the Understanding.* Edited, with Introduction,
Notes &c. by T. FOWLER, D.D. *Third Edition.* . [Extra fcap. 8vo, 2s. 6d.

Addison. *Selections from Papers in the ' Spectator.'* By T. ARNOLD, M.A. *Sixteenth Thousand.* . [Extra fcap. 8vo, 4s. 6d. *In Parchment, 6s.*

Steele. *Selected Essays from the Tatler, Spectator, and Guardian.* By AUSTIN DOBSON. . . . . [Extra fcap. 8vo. *In Parchment, 7s. 6d.*

Swift. *Selections from his Works.* Edited, with Life, Introductions, and Notes, by HENRY CRAIK. Two Vols. [Crown 8vo, cloth extra, price 15s. *Each volume may be had separately, price 7s. 6d.*

Pope. I. *Essay on Man.* Edited by MARK PATTISON, B.D. *Sixth Edition.* . . . . [Extra fcap. 8vo, 1s. 6d.

—— II. *Satires and Epistles.* By the same Editor. *Fourth Edition.* [Extra fcap. 8vo, 2s.

Thomson. *The Seasons,* and *The Castle of Indolence.* Edited by J. LOGIE ROBERTSON, M.A. . . . . . [Extra fcap. 8vo, 4s. 6d.

—— *The Castle of Indolence.* By the same Editor. [Extra fcap. 8vo, 1s. 6d.

Berkeley. *Selections.* With Introduction and Notes. By A. C. FRASER, LL.D. *Fourth Edition.* . . . . . [Crown 8vo, 8s. 6d.

Johnson. I. *Rasselas.* Edited, with Introduction and Notes, by G. BIRKBECK HILL, D.C.L. [Extra fcap. 8vo, *limp,* 2s.; *Bevelled boards,* 3s. 6d.; *in Parchment,* 4s. 6d.

—— II. *Rasselas; Lives of Dryden and Pope.* Edited by ALFRED MILNES, M.A. . . . . . . [Extra fcap. 8vo, 4s. 6d.

Lives of Dryden and Pope. . . [*Stiff covers,* 2s. 6d.

—— III. *Life of Milton.* Edited, with Notes, &c., by C. H. FIRTH, M.A. . . . [Extra fcap. 8vo, *stiff covers,* 1s. 6d.; *cloth,* 2s. 6d.

—— IV. *Vanity of Human Wishes.* With Notes, by E. J. PAYNE, M.A. . . . . [*Paper covers,* 4d.

Gray. *Selected Poems.* Edited by EDMUND GOSSE, M.A. [*In Parchment,* 3s.

—— *The same,* together with Supplementary Notes for Schools. By FOSTER WATSON, M.A. . . . . [Extra fcap. 8vo, *stiff covers,* 1s. 6d.

—— *Elegy, and Ode on Eton College.* . . . [*Paper covers,* 2d.

Goldsmith. *Selected Poems.* Edited, with Introduction and Notes, by AUSTIN DOBSON. . . [Extra fcap. 8vo, 3s. 6d. *In Parchment,* 4s. 6d.

—— *The Traveller.* Edited by G. B. HILL, D.C.L. [*Stiff covers,* 1s.

—— *The Deserted Village.* . . . . . [*Paper covers,* 2d.

Cowper. I. *The Didactic Poems of* 1782, with Selections from the Minor Pieces, A.D. 1779-1783. Edited by H. T. GRIFFITH, B.A. [Extra fcap. 8vo, 3s.

—— II. *The Task, with Tirocinium,* and Selections from the Minor Poems, A.D. 1784-1799. By the same Editor. [Extra fcap. 8vo, 3s.

Burke. I. *Thoughts on the Present Discontents; the two Speeches on America.* Edited by E. J. PAYNE, M.A. . . [Extra fcap. 8vo, 4s. 6a.

—— II. *Reflections on the French Revolution.* By the same Editor. *Second Edition.* . . . . . [Extra fcap. 8vo, 5s.

—— III. *Four Letters on the Proposals for Peace with the Regicide Directory of France.* By the same Editor. [Extra fcap. 8vo, 5s.

Burns. *Selected Poems.* Edited by J. LOGIE ROBERTSON, M.A.
[Crown 8vo, 6s.

Keats. *Hyperion,* Book I. With Notes, by W. T. ARNOLD, B.A. 4d.

Byron. *Childe Harold.* With Introduction and Notes, by H. F. TOZER, M.A. . . . . [Extra fcap. 8vo, 3s. 6d. *In Parchment,* 5s.

Shelley. *Adonais.* With Introduction and Notes. By W. M. ROSSETTI. . . . . [Crown 8vo, 5s.

Scott. *Lady of the Lake.* Edited, with Preface and Notes, by W. MINTO, M.A. With Map. . . . . [Extra fcap. 8vo, 3s. 6d.

———— *Lay of the Last Minstrel.* Edited by W. MINTO, M.A. With Map. . . . [Extra fcap. 8vo, *stiff covers,* 2s. *In Parchment,* 3s. 6d.

———— *Lay of the Last Minstrel.* Introduction and Canto I, with Preface and Notes, by W. MINTO, M.A. . . . . [*Paper covers,* 6d.

———— *Lord of the Isles.* Edited, with Introduction and Notes, by THOMAS BAYNE. . . . . [Extra fcap. 8vo, 3s. 6d.

———— *Marmion.* Edited by T. BAYNE. . [Extra fcap. 8vo, 3s. 6d.

Campbell. *Gertrude of Wyoming.* Edited, with Introduction and Notes, by H. MACAULAY FITZGIBBON, M.A. *Second Edition.* [Extra fcap. 8vo, 1s.

Wordsworth. *The White Doe of Rylstone.* Edited by WILLIAM KNIGHT, LL.D., University of St. Andrews. . . . [Extra fcap. 8vo, 2s. 6d.

Typical Selections *from the best English Writers. Second Edition.* In Two Volumes. . . . . . . [Extra fcap. 8vo, 3s. 6d. each.

HISTORY AND GEOGRAPHY, &c.

Freeman. *A Short History of the Norman Conquest of England.* By E. A. FREEMAN, M.A. *Third Edition.* . . [Extra fcap. 8vo, 2s. 6d.

Greswell. *History of the Dominion of Canada.* By W. PARR GRESWELL, M.A. . . . . [Crown 8vo, 7s. 6d.

———— *Geography of the Dominion of Canada and Newfoundland.* By the same Author. . . . . [Crown 8vo, 6s.

———— *Geography of Africa South of the Zambesi.* By the same Author. . . . . [Crown 8vo, 7s. 6d.

Hughes (Alfred). *Geography for Schools.* Part I, *Practical Geography.* With Diagrams. . . . . . . [Extra fcap. 8vo, 2s. 6d.

Hunter. *A Brief History of the Indian Peoples.* By Sir W. W. HUNTER, K.C.S.I. *Eighty-second Thousand.* . . . [Crown 8vo, 3s. 6d.

Kitchin. *A History of France.* With Numerous Maps, Plans, and Tables. By G. W. KITCHIN, D.D., Dean of Durham. *New Edition.* Vol. I. To 1453. Vol. II. 1453-1624. Vol. III. 1624-1793. Each 10s. 6d.

Lucas. *Introduction to a Historical Geography of the British Colonies.* By C. P. LUCAS, B.A. . . . [Crown 8vo, with 8 maps, 4s. 6d.

———— *Historical Geography of the British Colonies—*
   I. *The Mediterranean and Eastern Colonies* (exclusive of India).
[Crown 8vo, with 11 maps, 5s.
   II. *The West Indian Dependencies.* With 12 maps. . [7s. 6d.
   III. *West Africa.* With 5 maps. . . . . [7s. 6d.

MATHEMATICS AND PHYSICAL SCIENCE.

Aldis. *A Text Book of Algebra (with Answers to the Examples).* By W. Steadman Aldis, M.A. . . . . . [Crown 8vo, 7s. 6d.

Emtage. *An Introduction to the Mathematical Theory of Electricity and Magnetism.* By W. T. A. Emtage, M.A. . . [Crown 8vo, 7s. 6d.

Fisher. *Class-Book of Chemistry.* By W. W. Fisher, M.A., F.C.S Second Edition. . . . . [Crown 8vo, 4s. 6d.

Fock. *An Introduction to Chemical Crystallography.* By Andreas Fock, Ph.D. Translated and Edited by W. J. Pope. With a Preface by N. Story-Maskelyne, M.A., F.R.S. . . . . . [Crown 8vo, 5s.

Hamilton and Ball. *Book-keeping.* By Sir R. G. C. Hamilton, K.C.B., and John Ball. *New and Enlarged Edition.* [Extra fcap. 8vo, 2s. ⁎⁎* Ruled Exercise Books adapted to the above may be had, price 1s. 6d. ; also, adapted to the Preliminary Course only, price 4d.*

Harcourt and Madan. *Exercises in Practical Chemistry.* Vol. I. *Elementary Exercises.* By A. G. Vernon Harcourt, M.A., and H. G. Madan, M.A. *Fourth Edition.* Revised by H. G. Madan, M.A.
[Crown 8vo, 10s. 6d.

Hensley. *Figures made Easy: a first Arithmetic Book.* By Lewis Hensley, M.A. . . . . . [Crown 8vo, 6d. *Answers,* 1s.

——— *The Scholar's Arithmetic.* By the same Author.
[Crown 8vo, 2s. 6d. *Answers,* 1s. 6d.

——— *The Scholar's Algebra.* An Introductory work on Algebra. By the same Author. . . . . . . [Crown 8vo, 2s. 6d.

Nixon. *Euclid Revised.* Containing the essentials of the Elements of Plane Geometry as given by Euclid in his First Six Books. Edited by R. C. J. Nixon, M.A. *Third Edition.* . . . . . [Crown 8vo, 6s.

⁎⁎* May likewise be had in parts as follows—*

Book I, 1s. Books I, II, 1s. 6d. Books I–IV, 3s. Books V, VI, 3s. 6d.

——— *Geometry in Space.* Containing parts of Euclid's Eleventh and Twelfth Books. By the same Author. . . . [Crown 8vo, 3s. 6d.

——— *Elementary Plane Trigonometry ; that is, Plane Trigonometry without Imaginaries.* By the same Author. . . . [Crown 8vo, 7s. 6d.

Russell. *An Elementary Treatise on Pure Geometry.* By J. Wellesley Russell, M.A. . . . . [Crown 8vo, 10s. 6d.

Selby. *Elementary Mechanics of Solids and Fluids.* By A. L. Selby, M.A. . . . . [Crown 8vo, 7s. 6d.

Williamson. *Chemistry for Students.* By A. W. Williamson, Phil. Doc., F.R.S. . . . . . . [Extra fcap. 8vo, 8s. 6d.

Woollcombe. *Practical Work in General Physics.* For use in Schools and Colleges. By W. G. Woollcombe, M.A., B.Sc. . . [Crown 8vo, 3s.

——— *Practical Work in Heat.* By the same Author.
[Crown 8vo, 3s.

——— *Practical Work in Light and Sound.* By the same Author.
[Crown 8vo, 3s.

——— *Practical Work in Electricity and Magnetism.* [In Preparation.

Fowler. *The Elements of Deductive and Inductive Logic.* By T. FOWLER, D.D.   .   .   .   . [Extra fcap. 8vo, 7s. 6d.

Also, separately—

The Elements of Deductive Logic, designed mainly for the use of Junior Students in the Universities. With a Collection of Examples.
[Extra fcap. 8vo, 3s. 6d.

The Elements of Inductive Logic, designed mainly for the use of Students in the Universities. *Sixth Edition.* .   .   . [Extra fcap. 8vo, 6s.

Music.—Farmer. *Hymns and Chorales for Schools and Colleges.* Edited by JOHN FARMER, Organist of Balliol College.   .   .   .   . [5s.
☞ *Hymns without the Tunes,* 2s.

Hullah. *The Cultivation of the Speaking Voice.* By JOHN HULLAH.
[Extra fcap. 8vo, 2s. 6d.

Maclaren. *A System of Physical Education: Theoretical and Practical.* By ARCHIBALD MACLAREN. *New Edition,* re-edited and enlarged by WALLACE MACLAREN, M.A., Ph.D.   .   .   .   . [Crown 8vo, 8s. 6d. net.

Troutbeck and **Dale.** *A Music Primer for Schools.* By J. TROUTBECK, D.D., formerly Music Master in Westminster School, and R. F. DALE, M.A., B.Mus., late Assistant Master in Westminster School. [Crown 8vo, 1s. 6d.

Tyrwhitt. *A Handbook of Pictorial Art.* By R. St. J. TYRWHITT, M.A. With coloured Illustrations, Photographs, and a chapter on Perspective, by A. MACDONALD. *Second Edition.*   .   .   . [8vo, *half-morocco,* 18s.

Upcott. *An Introduction to Greek Sculpture.* By L. E. UPCOTT, M.A.   .   .   .   . [Crown 8vo, 4s. 6d.

Student's Handbook to the University and Colleges of Oxford. *Thirteenth Edition.*   .   .   .   . [Crown 8vo, 2s. 6d. net.

Helps to the Study of the Bible, taken from the *Oxford Bible for Teachers.* New, Enlarged and Illustrated Edition. Pearl 16mo, stiff covers, 1s. net. Large Paper Edition, Long Primer 8vo, cloth boards, 4s. 6d. net.

Helps to the Study of the Book of Common Prayer. Being a Companion to Church Worship.   .   .   .   .   . [Crown 8vo, 3s. 6d.

Old Testament History for Schools. By T. H. STOKOE, D.D.
Part   I.   From the Creation to the Settlement in Palestine.
Part II.   From the Settlement to the Disruption of the Kingdom.
[Extra fcap. 8vo, 2s. 6d. each.
Part III.   *In the Press.*

Notes on the Gospel of St. Luke; *for Junior Classes.* By E. J. MOORE SMITH. With Maps and Illustrations.   [Extra fcap. 8vo, 1s. 6d.

.*. A READING ROOM *has been opened at the* CLARENDON PRESS WAREHOUSE, AMEN CORNER, *where visitors will find every facility for examining old and new works issued from the Press, and for consulting all official publications.*

𝕷𝖔𝖓𝖉𝖔𝖓: HENRY FROWDE,
OXFORD UNIVERSITY PRESS WAREHOUSE, AMEN CORNER.
𝕰𝖉𝖎𝖓𝖇𝖚𝖗𝖌𝖍: 12 FREDERICK STREET.

www.ingramcontent.com/pod-product-compliance
Lightning Source LLC
Chambersburg PA
CBHW020545270326
41927CB00006B/732